Contents

Note on the Text

All quotations from the four poems are taken from *The Poems of the Pearl Manuscript*, ed. M. Andrew and R. Waldron (London, 1978), with distribution of u/v modernized, th for thorn, and gh, w, or y for yogh. Translations are my own. Quotations from the Bible are taken from the Douai translation of the Latin Vulgate, with occasional references to the Authorized Version (AV). The *Companion to the 'Gawain'-Poet*, ed. D. Brewer and J. Gibson (Woodbridge, 1997), is cited as *Companion*.

1

The Book and its Afterlife

Discussion of 'the *Gawain*-poet' must begin, not with a man, but with a book; for everything that is known about this writer (or writers) derives from a single manuscript volume, now in the British Library, London. It is a small book, less than five inches by seven, consisting of ninety leaves of parchment. It contains four poems, copied out by someone (not the poet) around the year 1400. This copyist writes a rather unusual small, sharp hand; and the dialect forms of his English locate his origins somewhere near the borders of Cheshire and Staffordshire, in the north-west of the English Midlands. Medieval manuscripts do not have title-pages, and this scribe provides no headings or paratext of any sort – just four plain poems. The titles of these have therefore been given by modern editors: *Pearl* is first, followed by *Cleanness* (sometimes called *Purity*), *Patience*, and finally *Sir Gawain and the Green Knight*. Originally the four texts were distinguished from each other simply by leaving blank parchment between; but an illustrator subsequently took advantage of these blanks, and of extra leaves at the beginning and end, to add twelve rather clumsy pictures illustrating the poems, something quite uncommon in the English manuscripts of the time. Subjects include the dreamer's encounter with the maiden in *Pearl*, Noah's Ark (*Cleanness*), Jonah being thrown into the sea (*Patience*), and the Green Knight at Arthur's court.[1]

Modern knowledge of medieval English literature is very patchy and imperfect, depending as it does upon the chances of survival of such copies as were made at the time. However, by the end of the fourteenth century increased demand for vernacular books was being met by increased production of copies, and English writings began to enjoy much improved chances of survival. Chaucer's *Canterbury Tales*, Gower's *Confessio*

1

Amantis, and Langland's *Piers Plowman* were all preserved in many copies, and so became available to early printers. Hence they could enter the general canon of English writings, where they have remained continuously, though not without ups and downs, from Tudor times to the present day. By contrast, the four anonymous poems under consideration here suffered a long period of obscurity and neglect. None of them survives in copies other than the manuscript in the British Library; and there is very little evidence that early readers knew them – little more than some apparent echoes of *Sir Gawain* in the verses of a Cheshire poet called Humphrey Newton (d. 1536) and a reworking of the story of the same poem in a fifteenth-century romance, *The Grene Knight*.[2] The surviving manuscript surely had its early readers (the name 'Hugo de' is written above the opening of *Sir Gawain*), but its first identifiable owner was a Yorkshire book-collector, Henry Savile of Banke (1568–1617), in whose catalogue it appears as 'An owld booke in English verse beginninge Perle plesant to Princes pay in 4°. Limned', citing the first line of the first poem, and defining the book as a quarto with illustrations. From Savile the book passed into the collection of Sir Robert Cotton (1586–1631), and from the Cotton collection into the British Museum, with the shelfmark MS Cotton Nero A. x (because the book had occupied the tenth place on the top shelf of a bookcase surmounted by a bust of the emperor Nero in Sir Robert's Westminster library). There it has remained, with the same shelfmark, to this day, in what is now the British Library.

So far as we know, this 'owld booke in English verse' lay largely undisturbed on the shelves of Cotton's library and the British Museum throughout the seventeenth and most of the eighteenth centuries. The first sign that its prolonged period of latency was coming to an end appears in the third volume (1781) of Thomas Warton's great *History of English Poetry*. In a footnote here, Warton printed twelve lines from an alliterative 'Vision on vellum' (*Pearl*), together with four lines from *Cleanness*, described as 'an alliterative poem without rhyme, exactly in the versification of Piers Plowman, of equal or higher antiquity'.[3] These are the first lines ever printed from the Cotton Nero poems. Nothing from *Sir Gawain* was to appear in print until 1824, when Richard Price, in his new edition of Warton's *History*, mentions in passing 'the discovery of the alliterative romance on the adventures of Sir Gawain' and gives a short specimen, again in a footnote.[4] The first complete edition of that poem, by Sir Frederic Madden, appeared fifteen years later, in 1839, with the encouragement of Sir Walter Scott, under Madden's pseudo-medieval title 'Syr Gawayn and the Grene Kny3t'; and this was followed in 1864 by the first edition of the other three poems, named by their editor, Richard Morris, 'Pearl', 'Cleanness', and 'Patience'. All four poems were now at last out in the public domain, and numerous later editors have built on the work of Madden and Morris. To begin with, readers' interests were mainly philological and antiquarian; but already Richard Morris had claimed that the poet (he thought there was only one) could 'stand in the foremost rank of England's early bards', and the poems gradually came to be more widely appreciated, despite the linguistic difficulties they present. *Pearl* and *Sir Gawain*, in particular, have been the object of many literary studies in the latter half of the twentieth century.

The same two poems have also prompted creative responses from artists, writers, and musicians. An edition of *Pearl* by Sir Israel Gollancz, published in 1891, has as its frontispiece a picture of the pearl-maiden by the Pre-Raphaelite artist Holman Hunt. It also includes some lines by Lord Tennyson, celebrating the recovery of the poem from obscurity:

> We lost you – for how long a time –
> True Pearl of our poetic prime!
> We found you, and you gleam reset
> In Britain's lyric coronet.

More remarkable is Douglas Oliver's recent long poem, *The Infant and the Pearl* (1985), a *tour de force* that matches the complex form of *Pearl*, with 101 twelve-line stanzas, linked by refrain words and rhymed (or rather pararhymed) according to the same pattern. Like *Pearl*, too, Oliver's dream vision has its painful root in the death of an infant. This small child is associated with a visionary pearl-maiden called 'Rosine', who offers the prospect of mercy and love to an England governed by her evil simulacrum, the pearly Thatcher, 'blessed Margaret'.[5]

It is *Sir Gawain and the Green Knight*, however, that has attracted most attention. Three films have been based upon it, including a serious and interesting version for Thames Television shown in 1991 (Williams, *Companion*, 389–92). In 1993 Iris Murdoch

3

published *The Green Knight*, a long novel set in contemporary London which takes the Middle English poem as its chief object of intertextual reference. Towards the end (p. 431), one of the characters, Clement, recalls reading a translation of the poem when he was an undergraduate; and Murdoch has him give a summary of the plot for the benefit of readers who may not know it. 'Pieces of the story are there,' Clement reflects, 'but aren't they somehow jumbled up and all the wrong way round?' Yet the Green Knight figure is clearly identified in the mysterious stranger Peter Mir with his green umbrella, who breaks in on the world of the Anderson family and their circle of friends. At the hands of one of them, Mir suffers an apparent death, from which he returns to exact a 'symbolic retribution' in the form of a superficial knife-cut. This replay of the poem's Beheading Game seems, in the end, to have done everyone good. Murdoch bases her conception of Mir on a somewhat romantic reading of the medieval original: 'After all, the Green Knight came out from some other form of being, weird and un-Christian, not like Arthur's knights. But he was noble and he knew what justice was' (p. 456). At about the same time, the composer Harrison Birtwhistle created his two-act opera *Gawain*, first staged at Covent Garden in 1991 and revived mostly recently in 2000. The libretto, by David Harsent, follows the original action quite closely; but it does not reproduce the Christian-chivalric ideology of the old poem: Arthur's court appears weak and trivial, and the hero is a north-country 'Gawain', never 'Sir Gawain'. The hero's winter ordeal is presided over from the start by Morgan le Fay, who draws him into the 'badlands of sleep', a nightmare journey to encounter death, from which he emerges stripped of all heroic pretensions. The libretto emphasizes the subjective, dream-like character of Gawain's experience by constant ritualistic repetitions and refrains. These are matched in the powerful, obsessive music, as in the arming scene at the end of Act I, or the three temptation scenes of Act II (Williams, *Companion*, 373–83).

Works such as Oliver's *The Infant and the Pearl*, Murdoch's *The Green Knight*, and especially Birtwhistle's *Gawain* serve to mark the final emergence of the two most remarkable Cotton Nero poems out of the obscurity to which the history of their manuscript for so long condemned them.

4

2

Pearl

Whoever put *Pearl* first in the Cotton Nero manuscript had good reason for giving it pride of place (if that was indeed the intention). To a reader of the time *Pearl* must have seemed the most up-to-date and adventurous of the four poems in the book. Technically it is very ambitious, with 101 long stanzas rhymed according to a demanding scheme and linked together by repeated words in groups of five. The poet handles the dream-vision form, fashionable at the time, with great virtuosity, especially in developing the symbolism of pearls. He also brings contemporary theological thought to bear on a private loss – the death of an infant not yet two years old – in an attempt to produce what might be described as a Consolation of Theology. The poem may even owe something to that most advanced of all fourteenth-century vernacular poems (little known in England at the time), Dante's *Divine Comedy*.

Pearl opens with a curious reversal of the expected relationship between waking experience and dream. In the first group of five stanzas, which form a waking prologue to the ensuing dream, the narrator describes how, one August day, he returned to a grassy place where he had previously dropped and lost a particularly fine pearl, and how at last he fell asleep there. That is what literally happens; but the events acquire a dreamlike strangeness in the telling, as the true source of the narrator's intense distress is enigmatically hinted at. A pearl that rots (l. 26) must be organic; and a pearl with slender, smooth sides (l. 6) sounds, in Middle English poetic language, like a woman; and it is women, not pearls, whose 'luf-daungere' (standoffishness or inaccessibility, l. 11) makes men suffer. So is the poem to be a love-allegory? What did the narrator in reality lose? The enigma is left unresolved until, in the dream, the loss is identified as a

5

paternal bereavement. The narrator there encounters his lost pearl as a female 'nearer to me than aunt or niece', he says (l. 233), who 'lived not two years on earth' (l. 483). These two clues, despite their somewhat evasive phrasing, are enough to settle the matter, when they are taken together. The occasion of the poem, shadowed in its waking prologue, was the death of a one-year-old daughter.

The baby girl is associated in the dream with a rich cluster of symbolic pearls, but she is not herself to be understood allegorically. So far as concerns the narrative, her death before reaching the age of two stands as a literal fact. This is not to say, of course, that the poem necessarily records an actual bereavement, suffered by the poet himself or by someone for whom he wrote. That may or may not be so: in the absence of documentary evidence, readers are free to decide for themselves or, if they prefer, ignore the question. However, comparison with other poems of the time tends to encourage a biographical interpretation. Thus, most people would agree that the Beatrice whom Dante encounters in his visions of purgatory and paradise represents the blessed spirit of an actual Florentine lady loved by the poet in life; and the visionary maiden Olympia who appears to Giovanni Boccaccio in the fourteenth of his Latin *Eclogues* is identified by Boccaccio himself, in a letter, as his daughter Violante, said to have died at the age of five and a half.[1] Nearer home, Chaucer's elegaic *Book of the Duchess* is known to have been occasioned by the death of Blanche, Duchess of Lancaster, in 1368. Furthermore, Chaucer's translation of the dead lady's actual name into the dream-name 'White' in that poem lends some support to the suggestion, hazarded by Gollancz in his edition of *Pearl*, that the dead girl had been christened Margery, for that name means 'pearl' (Latin *margarita*): pearls are called 'margarys' in the poem (ll. 199, 206, 1037).[2] Such play with personal names sometimes allowed older poets – Will Langland in *Piers Plowman*, Will Shakespeare in his *Sonnets* – to root their writings unobtrusively in the reality of their lives.

However this may be, *Pearl* takes very seriously the case which it addresses – the grief of a father who has lost a very young daughter, and the strangeness, for him, of thinking of her as dead. The strangeness arises chiefly from a reversal of normal

6

seniorities between father and daughter. The daughter has already experienced a great event, done a momentous thing, that has not yet come the father's way: she has died. So the pearl-maiden might say, as Olympia says to her father Boccaccio: 'I have done what you also will do in time to come' ('feci quod tu quoque, Silvi,|post facies', ll. 148–9). Any father at any time might feel something like awe in face of a child who has, as it were, outrun him by dying; but the poet's conception of the Christian afterlife endows his dead child with a more specific advantage over her father. For she is now one of the brides of Christ, blessed spirits who, as she says, 'thurghoutly haven cnawyng' – that is, understand everything completely (l. 859). As a disembodied spirit, she is freed from those limitations and distortions which prevent living people from understanding and knowing 'throughoutly'; so she enjoys a position of authority such as no living child could claim – least of all, in those days, a female child – and she speaks with that authority right through the long encounter with her father which occupies the greater part of his vision (ll. 161–976). Yet the dreamer himself cannot forget – how could he forget? – that he was, and still is, her father; and it is this recurrent failure to come to terms with their strange new relationship which generates much of the tension and pathos in their exchanges.

The tension is there from the start. When the dreamer first encounters his daughter, in the exotic supernatural landscape of his vision, it is not as a toddler but as a beautiful young woman in her full growth. She is 'at that time of life to which, we believe, citizens of heaven are assigned after death', as Boccaccio observes about his Olympia, explaining in a letter the discrepancy between the beautiful woman of his vision and the five-year-old child who died. The pearl-maiden sits, a dazzling vision of white and gold, at the foot of a crystal cliff, on the other side of that river which, throughout the dream, is to separate the narrator from the other world:

> More mervayle con my dom adaunt.
> I segh byyonde that myry mere
> A crystal clyffe ful relusaunt:
> Mony ryal ray con fro hit rere.
> At the fote therof ther sete a faunt,
> A mayden of menske, ful debonere;

7

Blysnande whyt watz hyr bleaunt;
I knew hyr wel, I hade sen hyr ere.
As glysnande golde that man con schere,
So schon that schene anunder schore.
On lenghe I loked to hyr there;
The lenger, I knew hyr more and more.

(ll. 157–68)

[A greater wonder overcame my mind; for I saw, on the other side of
that beautiful water, a crystal cliff reflecting from its surface much
bright light, and at its base sat a child, a gentle and very gracious
maiden, in a mantle of gleaming white. I knew her well, for I had seen
her before. She shone in her brightness, there under the cliff, like gold
that shines when it is first sliced. I gazed at her for a long time; and the
longer I looked, the more certainly I knew her.]

The dreamer can already speak of the woman as a child ('faunt'),
for he knows he has seen her before and becomes increasingly
sure that he knows who she is; yet she appears also as a 'mayden
of menske' – even, as the description proceeds, a queen, for she
wears a crown 'highe pynakled of cler quyt perle' (207). When
she appears to the dreamer, coming down to the water's edge to
greet him, she at first acts as a dutiful daughter might, bowing
low and taking off her crown as an act of respect. These gestures
confirm the dreamer's identification of her and prompt an
outburst of paternal feeling:

'O perle,' quoth I, 'in perlez pyght,
Art thou my perle that I haf playned,
Regretted by myn one on nyghte?'

(ll. 241–3)

['O pearl,' I say, 'adorned with pearls, are you my pearl that I have
mourned and lamented in the lonely nights?']

But the maiden, it turns out, is to make no further concessions to
the man's feelings as a father; and her response to his outburst
establishes the position which she is to hold for the rest of their
encounter:

That juel thenne in gemmez gente
Vered up her vyse with yyen graye,
Set on hyr coroun of perle orient,
And soberly after thenne con ho say:
'Sir, ye haf your tale mysetente...'

(ll. 253–7)

[Then that graciously begemmed jewel raised up her face with its gray eyes, replaced her crown of orient pearl, and went on to speak with great seriousness: 'Sir, you have spoken wrongly...']

Lifting up her lowered head and replacing her crown, she embarks on the first of her grave and uncompromising speeches of correction and reproof.

It has not proved easy for readers of the 'debate' that follows to settle their responses to either of the two interlocutors. In the case of the pearl-maiden, one is confronted by a blessed soul no longer capable of error, and now detached from all those human affections which were rooted in the body she has left behind. Such figures are not commonly encountered in stories, and even readers who share the poet's beliefs about the afterlife find it hard to sympathize with the maiden's treatment of her father. She is, certainly, concerned for his spiritual welfare, but she signally fails to respond to his attempts to invoke their former emotional attachment. She also corrects his various mistaken notions with the uncompromising severity of one who knows the truth 'throughoutly', as when she speaks of the three distinct errors he has just foolishly committed (ll. 290–300). In these respects, she resembles Beatrice in the *Divine Comedy*. The very first words spoken by Beatrice to Dante there leave him abashed: 'She seemed haughty to me, like a mother to her son; for the taste of harsh pity [*pietade acerba*] has a bitterness about it' (*Purgatorio*, XXX, ll. 79–81). It is important to appreciate the absoluteness of the truth for which, like Beatrice, the pearl-maiden is held to stand; yet her 'harsh pity' for the dreamer does not mark him as contemptible or ridiculous, as some have supposed. Certainly, his inability to grasp lofty and sometimes paradoxical truths shows him to be subject to the limitations of human understanding; but could any human being have been expected to understand? His questions and objections may seem unduly literal-minded; but they match the literal mode in which the vision displays spiritual realities to him. 'How can you be a queen?' seems not at all an unreasonable question in face of a woman visibly wearing a crown (ll. 421–32); and his later question about where she lives hardly seems foolish once it has been answered by his actual sight of her home, the Heavenly Jerusalem as described, in some physical detail, by St John in the Book of Revelation. Few educated people in the Middle Ages thought that heaven was really like that; but the *Pearl*-poet would have realized that his poem, like the Book of Revelation, had to accommodate invisible things to the limited capacities of human understanding – as represented, not altogether unfairly, by the dreamer in his encounter with a blessed soul.[3]

In a Latin letter about the *Divine Comedy* addressed to Can Grande, probably by Dante himself, the writer explains what he calls the 'form of treatment' (*forma tractandi*) adopted in that poem: 'The form or method of treatment is poetic, fictive, descriptive, digressive, and figurative; and it also employs definition, analysis, proof, refutation, and the setting forth of examples'.[4] In modern times we expect poems to be poetic, fictive, and figurative; but we hardly look to them for definitions, analyses, proofs, or refutations. Yet *Pearl*, like the *Comedy*, does set out to demonstrate certain truths, both to the narrator and to the reader. The demonstrations rest directly on biblical texts – the safest foundations for theological proof – and they concern God's rewards in the afterlife; for the dreamer wants to know 'where his pearl has gone' (cf. l. 376). Since she has been cleansed of the inherited stain of original sin by baptism, and did not live long enough thereafter to sin on her own behalf, she died as an innocent, one of those children of whom Jesus said 'of such is the kingdom of God' (Luke 18: 16, cited at ll. 718–19). Yet, although one can hardly imagine that God would condemn such a guiltless soul (ll. 667–8), there remains a difficulty. What about all those other people who may be said to have earned their heavenly rewards by a lifetime of struggle? What, the dreamer almost asks, about me? Is it fair that the dead child should gain those rewards so quickly and easily – indeed, after doing nothing at all to deserve them? This objection, voiced by the dreamer, is met by the maiden telling Christ's Parable of the Vineyard (ll. 497–572). The events of the parable are vividly imagined, in a 'poetic, fictive, descriptive' mode; but the story has a definite point to prove, for it identifies innocents like the pearl-maiden with those who did least work in the vineyard, the late-comers who 'wroght not hourez two' (l. 555, for 'hours' read 'years') and yet immediately received the same 'penny' as those who worked all day. The protests of the other workers in the story are echoed by the dreamer, who objects to the outcome as 'unreasonable', citing Psalm 61 (AV 62), verse 13:

10

'thou wilt render to every man according to his works' (ll. 590–600). The maiden replies that 'more and less' are not at issue in the kingdom of heaven, where a generous God satisfies everyone alike –

> 'For ther is uch man payed inlyche,
> Whether lyttel other much be hys rewarde.'
>
> (ll. 603–4)

The interpretation of these lines is disputed, but I take them to mean that every blessed soul is equally satisfied or fulfilled ('payed' in a Middle English sense), even though the rewards they actually receive, judged by some objective standard, will vary according to their varying capacities for spiritual experience. The poet here is wrestling, as Langland does on occasion in *Piers Plowman*, with formidable problems about the justice of God's system of rewards and punishments. His solution (if I have understood lines 603–4 correctly) allows him to conclude the dream section of the poem with the narrator's vision of the Heavenly Jerusalem, where he sees 'his little queen' as one of the élite corps of virgins accompanying the Lamb of God. These are the 144,000 *virgines* seen by St John in Chapter 14 of the Book of Revelation – the same privileged company that is joined after death by the little 'innocent' of Chaucer's *Prioress's Tale* (*Canterbury Tales*, VII, ll. 579–85). I share the disappointment that most readers feel when the dream section ends the way it does, with a lengthy description of the Heavenly Jerusalem, taken avowedly and in detail from chapters of Revelation; but here, as in the Vineyard section, the 'probative' power of the verse depends upon its closeness to its authoritative source; and the demands of proof are sometimes at odds with the demands of poetry, here as in the *Divine Comedy*.

For all its undoubted set towards proof and refutation, *Pearl* could hardly be more unlike a theological treatise. It is, indeed, almost overpoweringly 'poetic' in those features by which poetry distinguishes itself from other forms of discourse: metrical and structural form, imagery, language. The poem would have appealed to the taste of the age for luxury items, not only because it abounds in references to precious stones and metals, but also because it is itself so evidently the product of many hours of skilled work by the 'jeweller' who created it.[5]

Metrically, *Pearl* differs greatly from *Patience* and *Cleanness*, and from most of *Gawain*, for these employ the unrhymed long alliterative line (see Chapter 3 here). *Pearl* itself is sometimes referred to as an alliterative poem, but wrongly so. Many of its lines do carry alliteration, sometimes heavy ('Perle plesaunte to prynces paye'); but this is not a condition of metricality, as in alliterative verse proper: about a quarter of the lines have no alliteration. Nor do *Pearl*'s lines conform to the rhythmical patterns of the long alliterative line, as found elsewhere in the manuscript. They are best read as rather free versions (in the scribal copy, at least) of the octosyllabic line, having four iambic feet (*Companion*, 232–7). They are organized into twelve-line stanzas, in a form that places heavy demands on a skill more highly valued in the Middle Ages than it is today: the art of 'rymyng craftily', as Chaucer calls it (*Canterbury Tales*, II, l. 48). Such very long 'ballade stanzas', here rhyming ababababbcbc, were fashionable in the England of Richard II.[6] Furthermore, because the stanzas form groups of five linked by the same word ending each, every group has to find six c-rhymes: in the first group of five stanzas, for instance, the refrain word 'spot' rhymes with 'yot', 'clot', 'not', 'flot', and 'schot'. The refrain word also acts as a further link between stanzas in a group. Having formed the rhyme at the end of one stanza, it recurs in the first line of the next: thus, the first stanza of the poem ends 'Of that pryvy perle withouten spot', to be followed at the beginning of the next stanza by 'Sythen in that spote hit fro me sprange'. The device also serves to link the five-stanza groups to each other; for the opening line of each will contain the refrain word from the previous group, making its last appearance there in that role. The same device – known as 'concatenation', or chaining together – is even employed to connect together the links which would otherwise hang loose, in the poem's first and last lines: the refrain word of the last group of stanzas, 'pay', appears at the beginning of the first, joining the poem back upon itself in a kind of circle.

One function of such formal devices was to ensure the integrity of the text, for this was a time when a scribe in the act of copying might omit or misplace parts; but some of the devices also contribute meanings to the poem, by virtue of the symbolic power then attributed to numbers and shapes. The number of lines in each stanza, twelve, proves to be significant, for the Heavenly Jerusalem, as described by St John and seen by the dreamer, is constructed on a module of twelve: twelve gates (l. 1035), twelve foundations (ll. 992–3), and the whole city a cube of twelve furlongs in every direction (ll. 1029–31; Revelation 21: 16 has 12,000 furlongs here). Furthermore, the dreamer sees his pearl-maiden in a company of 144,000 brides of the Lamb (ll. 786, 869–70), a number which can be thought of as twelve squared and raised to a higher power. Such cultivation of the number twelve may even help to explain one surprising irregularity in the formal structure of the poem. There are twenty stanza-groups, each of which contains five stanzas except only the fifteenth group, which has six (ll. 841–912). This has the effect of raising the total number of lines in the poem from 1200 to 1212, reduplicating, as it were, the heavenly number twelve. There is a similar effect in *Sir Gawain* (see below, p. 52). The extra stanza also raises the total number of stanzas from 100 to 101, as if to reinforce the effect of circularity created by the linking refrain word, with a suggestion of starting to go round again, perhaps endlessly. It is not that the poet expected that kind of devotion from a reader, as James Joyce did when segueing straight from the end to the beginning of *Finnegans Wake*; his intention was rather, I think, to match the symbolism of the pearl, rather oddly described as 'endelez rounde' (l. 738), in the roundness of his poem – whether or not readers noticed the effect (medieval scribes did not commonly number lines or stanzas).

The symbolism of the pearl itself receives very elaborate treatment in the poem, drawing on two main biblical sources. The first of these is already lurking behind the narrative, in the waking prologue, of a man who has lost his pearl in a grassy place. This rather odd situation recalls a closely linked pair of short parables, where Christ speaks of heaven: 'The kingdom of heaven is like unto a treasure hidden in a field. Which a man having found, hid it: and for joy thereof goeth and selleth all he hath and buyeth that field. Again the kingdom of heaven is like to a merchant seeking good pearls. Who, when he had found one pearl of great price, went his way and sold all that he had and bought it' (Matthew 13: 44–6). These two parables (some-times conflated by medieval readers) together outline a narrative of loss and recovery: the treasure hidden in the field and the pearl are both 'found' and purchased, by the man and the merchant, after selling all they had. In the poem, the jeweller first finds what he has lost in the field when he encounters the maiden: ' "O perle," quoth I, "in perlez pyght, | Art thou my perle that I haf playned?" ' When he addresses her as a 'perle', here and elsewhere, he is not using a personal name (the word should not be capitalized by editors); rather, he simply identifies her, in the poem's symbolic narrative, with his lost gem. Yet the pearls with which she is bedecked have what would then have been called a further anagogical sense, signifying the kingdom of heaven, as in Christ's parable. This is made explicit much later, when the maiden explains the meaning of the 'wonder perle' that she wears on her breast:

> 'This makellez perle that boght is dere,
> The joueler gef fore alle hys god,
> Is lyke the reme of hevenesse clere –
> So sayde the Fader of folde and flode –
> For it is wemlez, clene, and clere,
> And endelez rounde, and blythe of mode,
> And commune to alle that ryghtwys were.
> Lo, even inmyddez my breste hit stode.'

(ll. 733–40)

[This matchless pearl, so dearly bought, for which the jeweller gave all he had, is likened unto the bright kingdom of heaven, as the creator of land and sea declared; for it is flawless, pure, and bright, round without any end, joyous in itself, and common to all the righteous. See, it is hung right between my breasts.]

This parabolic identification of the pearl with the kingdom of heaven is reinforced later in the dreamer's vision of the heavenly city with its twelve gates of pearl (ll. 1037–8), as described in the Book of Revelation (21: 21): 'And the twelve gates are twelve pearls, one to each: and every several gate was of one several pearl'. But neither of these scriptural passages, as they stood, provided the poet with the further moral, or 'tropological', meanings which also attach to his pearls. Here, as in the exposition of another 'endless' symbol, Gawain's pentangle, arguments from authority are supplemented with arguments drawn directly from the nature of things. Because pearls are white and seamlessly spherical, they can be understood to symbolize absolute moral purity or innocence: either the baptismal innocence which the pearl-maiden had no occasion to lose, or the recovered purity of those who may 'receive the kingdom of God as a child' (ll. 722–4, Luke 18: 17) after a lifetime. The image of the pearl is applied specifically to the latter state in a passage in *Cleanness* (ll. 1113–32), where the round, white stone stands for the condition which adults can achieve through the polishing and washing processes of penance. That is the cost, for an adult such as the dreamer in *Pearl*, of buying that pearl of great price for which the merchant of the parable sold all he had.

The luxuriant symbolism of precious stones and metals in *Pearl*, supported though it is by the Book of Revelation, presents something of a challenge to modern taste; but a more difficult critical issue concerns the character of the writing, as one encounters it line by line. Unlike the other poems in the manuscript, *Pearl* subjects itself to extreme formal constraints, imposed upon its short lines by a difficult rhyme scheme and by the repetition of refrain words. It is one of those medieval poems – more common in Latin than in vernaculars – which stand at the opposite extreme from 'free' verse. One might describe it as 'bound', and tightly so. It is therefore not surprising, perhaps, that editors and readers alike sometimes find difficulty in justifying the poet's use of words, on occasions where strict formal requirements appear to have forced an unsuitable word, or a word in a strained sense, into the text. Judgement in such cases presents difficulties, partly because poets must be allowed certain liberties, but mainly because we now are not native speakers of late fourteenth-century English. In their glossaries, editors will record whatever sense of a word seems to be required in such contexts, and the dictionaries will then in their turn report it as one of the senses of the Middle English word. But where, as may happen in such cases, the dictionaries record no examples outside *Pearl* itself, the problem remains. What, for instance, would a competent fourteenth-century reader have made of the use of the word 'clot' at line 789, where the hill of Sion is referred to as 'that semly clot'? Elsewhere the poet applies the word to the earth in which bodies are buried, in perfect accord with Middle English usage (*Middle English Dictionary*, under *clot*, sense 1(b)); but the lexicographers are embarrassed by line 789, for which they find

15

no parallel, glossing the word there 'a hill or ? mound' (*Oxford English Dictionary*), or 'a (? grass-grown) knoll' (*Middle English Dictionary*). It seems that here, as on occasion elsewhere, the demands of the sixfold b-rhyme have simply proved too much. Cases of the same sort may also be found, as one might expect, among the refrain words, notably the word 'date' as it is used in the ninth group of stanzas.

We might prefer it if the poet had allowed himself rather more elbow-room, as Douglas Oliver has done by employing para-rhyme instead of strict rhyme in his *Infant and the Pearl*; but in fact the strictness of *Pearl*'s form produces more beauties than blemishes. Even simple lines, when they are read in their context, can acquire a distinctive air of grace under pressure. Examples are: 'I segh hyr in so strange a place' (l. 175), 'And quen mad on the fyrst day!' (l. 486), 'Thay wente into the vyne and wroghte' (l. 525), 'The sunne watz doun and hit wex late' (l. 538), and 'Then sagh I ther my lyttel quene' (l. 1147). Elsewhere, in lines of a richer texture, the effect may be one of dense and concentrated lyricism, as when the maiden's crown is described as 'Highe pynakled of cler quyt perle' (l. 207). There are two particularly exquisite similes of this kind. One compares the precious stones gleaming on the bed of the otherworld river to stars in winter:

> As stremande sternez, quen strothe-men slepe,
> Staren in welkyn in wynter nyght.
>
> (ll. 115–16)

[As streaming stars, when earthmen sleep, stare in the sky on a winter's night.]

Another simile introduces the mysterious manifestation of a procession of virgins in the heavenly city:

> Ryght as the maynful mone con rys
> Er thenne the day-glem dryve al doun,
> So sodanly on a wonder wyse
> I watz war of a prosessyoun.
>
> (ll. 1093–6)

[Just as the mighty moon will rise before the last light of day has sunk, so suddenly and wonderfully I became aware of a procession.]

It seems that the poem's formal structure has itself inspired this last remarkable comparison, for it occurs at the beginning of a

16

new stanza group where the word 'moon' is dictated by its occurrence as the refrain word of the previous group. Poets testify that such technical requirements can prompt unforeseen felicities; and the *Pearl*-poet certainly exploits what Charles Tomlinson has called 'the chances of rhyme'. The b-rhyming 'luf-daungere' must have struck him as a happy find, towards the end of the first stanza; and the adjective 'blue' works wonderfully well in the dreamer's incredulous question to the maiden, 'Art thou the quene of hevenez blwe?'; for blue is the colour, not only of the dreamer's earthly sky, but also of the Queen of Heaven herself, Mary, to whom he then refers (ll. 423–6). Repetitions of refrain words may cause difficulties, as I have suggested in the case of 'date'; but they can also create powerful effects, as in the prayer with which the poem concludes:

> He gef uus to be His homly hyne
> Ande precious perlez unto His pay.
>
> (ll. 1211–12)

[May he grant us to serve in his household and be precious pearls to his pleasure.]

The refrain word 'pay' points back to the beginning of the very first stanza group (where 'precious perles' also occur, at ll. 36, 48, and 60); and by doing so it serves to measure, as it were, the distance the poem has travelled since its first 'Perle plesaunte to pryces paye'.

The peculiar intricacy of *Pearl* invites comparison with the funerary monuments of the time, when tombs and chantry chapels commonly carried architectural elaboration to lengths unusual even by late Gothic standards. Such extravagantly decorated monuments might be seen, following Freud, as prompted by the painful feeling that the mourner himself is to blame for the loss of the loved object; for expenditure lavished on the departed – whether of time, skill, or money – would help to relieve the guilt of survivors and so advance what Freud called 'the work of mourning'.[7] Perhaps the creation of *Pearl* itself performed something like that function for the author, or for a father who commissioned it as a textual monument. However this may be, the poem does concern itself centrally, in the person of the dreamer, with the 'work of mourning'. *Pearl* sees the proper end of this work as a recognition of loss and a yielding up of possession, while fully recognizing how painful and difficult that process must be. The dream opens with two false starts. At first, the dreamer simply 'forgets all grief' (l. 86), as he moves through the bright fantastic landscape in which he finds himself. Then, encountering the pearl-maiden, he supposes that he has recovered her, and accordingly imagines a renewed life for them together (ll. 279–88). Yet the loss is real, and it can neither be forgotten nor denied; and for the rest of the dream the maiden struggles to convince her father that he can no longer possess her as 'my pearl'. At no time in the dream itself, however, does the father succeed in giving her up. The maiden's explanations, stressing the absolute otherness of her present existence beyond the grave, are all prompted by questions which themselves persistently betray parental concern and even, on occasion, parental reproach: 'Where do you live?', 'How *can* you be a queen?' Even when confronted with his final vision of the New Jerusalem, the dreamer still sees with a father's eye. He first notices the procession of virgins there as dressed 'in the same gyse | That watz my blysful anunder croun' (ll. 1099–1100); and he later identifies her among them as 'my lyttel quene' (l. 1147). Touching as these possessive pronouns are, their possessiveness serves to anticipate the dreamer's final lapse into incomprehension, when the sight of his little queen fills him with such love-longing that he moves to plunge into the stream that separates them – and wakes up.

When fourteenth-century dream poems arrive at their waking conclusions, narrators such as Will in *Piers Plowman* or Geoffrey in *The Parliament of Fowls* make little claim to have learned from what they dreamed; and the closing stanzas of *Pearl* are also somewhat muted. Far from finding himself joyfully consoled when he first wakes, the father still suffers from his old painful feelings. He becomes dismayed, sighs, swoons from 'longing', and cries out in distress (ll. 1174–81). Nor does he speak as someone completely persuaded by theological argument or mystical vision:

> If hit be veray and soth sermoun
> That thou so strykez in garlande gay,
> So wel is me in thys doel-doungoun
> That thou art to that Prynsez paye.

> (ll. 1185–8)

[If it is indeed true that you go thus in your bright garland, then it is a source of joy to me in this dungeon of sorrow that you have commended yourself to that prince's pleasure.]

It might seem that we are almost back in the poem's opening scene, where the father's 'wreched wylle in wo ay wraghte' (l. 56); but this is not the case, for he does now find himself newly able to submit his 'wretched will' to the will of God. As he says: 'Now al be to that Pryncez paye' (l. 1176). Such submission represents the very essence of the virtue patience, as this is to be explored and celebrated in the poem of that name later in the manuscript. There, the story of Jonah illustrates exactly what the father in *Pearl* finally learns to recognize: 'Lorde, mad hit arn that agayn The stryven' (l. 1199). Accordingly, the father can end by solemnly committing his pearl to God 'in Krystes dere blessyng and myn'. That is a formula which commonly occurs in letters addressed by medieval parents to their children, so the father here still speaks as a parent, touchingly, when he couples his paternal blessing with Christ's; but the formula belongs at the end of letters, and it mainly functions here as a perhaps definitive farewell.

3

Alliterative Poetry:
An Interchapter

The verse of *Pearl*, as has been said, belongs to that type of octosyllabic, four-stress poetry to be found also among the works of poets such as Chaucer and Milton; but the other three poems in the manuscript belong to a different metrical tradition, less familiar in modern times and therefore requiring some explanation here. They all employ the longer, unrhymed alliterative line throughout (except for the 'bob and wheel' with which each paragraph of *Sir Gawain* ends) and so form part of what some modern scholars call the Alliterative Revival.[1]

The metrical tradition to which *Pearl* belongs, along with most post-medieval English verse, had its origins in medieval Latin and French writings; but alliterative verse originated, not in Romania, but in Germania. The Anglo-Saxon peoples who colonized Britain in the fifth century brought with them a common Germanic tradition of verse-making, and all the poetry that survives from England before the Norman Conquest exhibits these already well-established techniques: Old English verse is all 'alliterative'. After the Conquest, however, this ancient native tradition had to compete increasingly with new international and especially French ways of composing poetry; and for about three hundred years after 1066 the record of alliterative verse is thin and patchy, so much so that one might have expected it to die out altogether. Yet, surprisingly, a very large body of alliterative verse survives from late medieval England, composed from about the middle of the fourteenth century until the beginning of the sixteenth. Literary historians have not had much success in explaining this apparent revival of an old way of writing verse; and little is known about the poets involved, most of whom remain anonymous (Langland being the chief exception). The majority of these writers must, on the evidence of their dialects, have originated away from London and the south-east: Langland in the west country, the Cotton Nero poet(s) in the north-west Midlands. In Chaucer's *Canterbury Tales*, the Parson says 'I am a Southren man; | I kan nat geeste "rum, ram, ruf" by lettre' (X 42–3). This only makes sense if southern men (Chaucer himself included) were not expected to produce 'rum, ram, ruf'. Looking out from London, Chaucer evidently saw alliterative verse as belonging elsewhere; but there is no reason to think that he shared his Parson's contempt for it: that rather puritanical cleric has no time for literature of any kind, and he dismisses 'rym' as little better than 'rum, ram, ruf'.

As his imitation of it in the course of the *Knight's Tale* shows, Chaucer knew some alliterative verse (though probably not the Cotton Nero poems), and the Parson's reference to 'rum, ram, ruf' is accurate enough, so far as it goes; for the standard line will have three words alliterating together (*Companion*, 221–32). These serve to bind into one the two halves into which each line divides, with two words in the first half-line alliterating with one in the second, thus: 'His clannes and his cortaysye croked were never'. For it to count metrically, alliteration must normally fall on stressed syllables, of which there are four in this kind of line, two in each half. A general rule, to which there are few exceptions, requires alliteration in the second half-line to fall on the first, and only the first, of its two stresses (as is also the rule in Old English verse). The first half-line is more variable, and may have three stressed syllables. Two of these must alliterate, but three of them may, as in the line 'The borgh brittened and brent to brondez and askez'.[2] Whereas the number of stressed syllables in a line is thus restricted to four or five, there is no overall count of unstressed syllables; so terms such as 'octosyllabic' are not applicable. Also, the distribution of unstressed syllables in relation to the stresses is very variable, even to the avoidance of regular patterns such as the iambic beat familiar in much non-alliterative poetry. Thus, the line first quoted above ('His clannes...') runs as follows: x/xxx/xx | /xx/x, and the second ('The borgh...') runs x//xx/ | x/xx/x. Each half-line is independent of its neighbour in its pattern, creating an effect of continuous variation in the rhythmical flow.

The diction and style of fourteenth-century alliterative verse differ from what one finds in Chaucer or Gower. In meeting the demands of alliteration itself, poets drew on sets of specialized poetic alternative words for common items such as 'man' or 'go'. The three Cotton Nero poems, for instance, use the following distinctively poetic words when referring to male persons: 'burne', 'hathel', 'lede', 'schalk', 'segge', 'tulk', 'wye'. These were not exact synonyms, but the choice between them was largely determined by the requirements of alliteration. Thus, if Sir Gawain was to ride through the realm of Logres, it is convenient to refer to him as a 'renk': 'Now ridez this renk thurgh the ryalme of Logres'; but when he sees his blood blink on the snow, he is a 'burne': 'And quen the burne segh the blode blenk on the snawe'. Poets also drew upon traditional expressions for the construction of half-lines. In the first half-line, where two alliterating sounds are required, one finds certain pairs of words, or 'collocations', commonly providing them. Thus, the word 'ryse' is coupled with the adverb 'radly' ('promptly') seven times in *Cleanness*, *Patience*, and *Gawain*: 'With that thay ros up radly...', 'Thenne he ryses radly...', 'And he ful radly upros...'. There are also less obvious forms of patterning in both first and second half-lines, even at the very abstract level where particular types of half-line rhythm are associated with particular patterns of syntax and grammar ('grammetrical patterns'). As Duggan puts it: 'The poets' choice of words as well as of their order and placement was determined partly by what they wished to say, partly by considerations of alliterative collocations, and partly by rhythmic concerns' (*Companion*, 230).

The half-line is the primary unit of alliterative verse. Neither manuscripts nor modern editions commonly mark the caesura dividing the line into two, and there is rarely much call to do so, for most half-lines coincide with units of syntax and sense and so can be easily identified: 'Now ridez this renk thurgh the ryalme of Logres'. The line-ends, too, commonly coincide with such phrasal boundaries, as the punctuation of modern editions indicates, and strong enjambement is rare. So the overall effect is one of a continuous string of half-lines, linked in pairs by alliteration, but subject to no higher formal constraints.

Strangely enough, however, the texts of *Cleanness* and *Patience* are divided up by the Cotton Nero scribe into four-line sections, marked off by a double oblique line in the left-hand margin; and some editors, accordingly, print these poems in four-line stanzas. These divisions commonly coincide with larger units of sense, perhaps reflecting a desire on the part of the poet himself to impose some extra formal control on the unregulated flow of the long lines; but they have no metrical significance and cannot properly be considered stanzas, let alone quatrains.[3] More significant is the use in *Sir Gawain* of the so-called 'bob and wheel', consisting of a single iambic foot (the 'bob') rhyming with a following quatrain of short lines (the 'wheel'). These serve regularly to mark off, and often clinch, paragraphs of unrhymed, long-line narrative – a device unparallelled elsewhere. The paragraphs vary greatly in length (from 12 long lines to 37) and again cannot properly be called stanzas; but it seems to be more than a coincidence that, like the stanzas in *Pearl*, they number 101.

4

Cleanness

The poem which follows *Pearl* in the Cotton Nero manuscript
presents a number of peculiar difficulties, including, for editors,
the problem of what to call it. In the very first line, it announces
its subject: 'clannesse'. 'Clene', 'clanly', and 'clannesse' do
indeed recur throughout as keywords; yet they cover a range
of meanings which the same words in modern English cannot
match. They denote in the poem a variety of physical properties,
including freedom from dirt on such things as clothes and
dishes, smoothness of surface, and high polish; but they also
denote a variety of moral and spiritual conditions, including
freedom from sexual sin. Richard Morris, the first editor of the
poem, called it 'Cleanness', a decision followed by most recent
scholars. However, that title, for a modern reader, leans heavily
towards the physical meanings. The alternative, adopted by
Menner in his excellent 1920 edition, is to call the poem 'Purity';
but here the modern word leans too far towards the moral and
spiritual side. This is more than a mere dilemma for editors:
their terminological difficulty reflects the fact that the poem
displays a particular complex of interrelated ideas, physical and
moral, which has largely broken up in modern times. Indeed,
some recent critics, as we shall see, have turned to the
anthropologists in order to make sense of it. In the circum-
stances, for lack of a properly comprehensive term, one might as
well follow the poet's own usage, and that generally favours the
vernacular 'clean' and its derivatives rather than the Franco-
Latin 'pure'. 'Cleanness' does, as a title, sound odder than
'Purity'; but then the poem itself is rather odd.

    Cleanness differs from the other poems in the manuscript most
of all in its structure. *Pearl, Patience,* and *Sir Gawain* all confine

themselves strictly to a single, continuous sequence of events; but *Cleanness* attempts no such unity of action. It draws upon the Bible for a number of distinct stories, taking narrative examples mainly from the Old Testament to illustrate its argument. These biblical episodes are selected to display God as a preserver and destroyer of men, and most especially as the destroyer of those who behave 'uncleanly'. The three central stories are: Noah's flood, Sodom and Gomorrah, and Belshazzar's feast. In each of these, God is shown destroying the unclean, while preserving those who win his favour (Noah himself and his family, Abraham and Lot, and even – surprisingly – Nebuchadnezzar). In his summary at the very end of the text, the poet plainly states the double point of these three examples, and of the poem as a whole:

> Thus upon thrynne wyses I haf yow thro schewed
> That unclannes tocleves in corage dere
> Of that wynnelych Lorde that wonyes in heven,
> Entyses Hym to be tene, teldes up His wrake;
> And clannes is His comfort, and coyntyse He lovyes,
> And those that seme arn and swete schyn se His face.

(ll. 1805–10)

[Thus I have clearly shown you in three ways how uncleanness breaks the precious heart of that gracious lord who dwells in heaven, provokes him to anger, and arouses him to inflict punishment; for cleanness is what he delights in, and he loves fine clothing, and those who are seemly and pleasing will see his face.]

The three examples referred to here occupy about two-thirds of the whole; but they are set within a matrix consisting of some ancillary stories and the author's reflections on his theme.

The poem starts with a series of reflections leading into the first biblical example. This prologue (ll. 1–204) speaks of God's love for cleanness and his rewards for those who are clean, citing the Beatitude 'Blessed are the clean of heart: for they shall see God' (Matthew 5: 8); but the heavier stress falls on God's hatred of uncleanness, 'fylthe'. Here the poet introduces the first of his ancillary narratives, a retelling of Christ's parable of the wedding feast, combining and elaborating the two scriptural versions, Matthew 22: 1–14 and Luke 14: 16–24. Just as in *Pearl*'s retelling of the parable of the vineyard, this extensive and vivid version (ll. 51–160) does nothing to soften the hard edge of its original; for the emphasis falls on the punishment of the man who, in Matthew's version, turns up at the feast improperly dressed. The poet interprets this man's 'wedez so fowle' as signifying moral uncleanness; and he goes on to observe that, although there are many kinds of sin, none provokes God as much as 'fylthe of the flesch' (l. 202).

It is this rather extraordinary proposition – not at all in line with most medieval thinking – that governs the first of the main stories, that of Noah's flood, told as an extreme example of God's angry reaction to human 'fylthe'. He had not previously been moved to fury, the poet observes, by his rebel angels, nor by the disobedience of Adam and Eve; and on both those occasions his punishment was moderate and restrained (falling short, that is, of utter destruction); but he showed no mercy on mankind in the time of Noah. The poet draws here upon a passage from Genesis, as that was understood in the Middle Ages:

> The sons of God seeing the daughters of men, that they were fair, took to themselves wives of all which they chose . . . Now giants were upon the earth in those days. For after the sons of God went in to the daughters of men, and they brought forth children, these are the mighty men of old, men of renown. And God seeing that the wickedness of men was great on the earth, and that all the thought of their heart was bent upon evil at all times, it repented him that he had made man on the earth. And being touched inwardly with sorrow of heart, he said: 'I will destroy man, whom I have created'.
> (Genesis 6: 2–7)

Following one medieval commentary tradition, the poet understands these mysterious 'sons of God' as fallen angels, sleeping as incubuses with human women; but he also found in commentaries the non-biblical idea that these devils were attracted to earth by the already corrupted sexuality of men and women:

> And thenne founden thay fylthe in fleschlych dedez,
> And controeved agayn kynde contraré werkez,
> And used hem unthryftyly uchon on other,
> And als with other, wylsfully, upon a wrange wyse:
> So ferly fowled her flesch that the fende loked
> How the deghter of the douthe wern derelych fayre
> And fallen in felaghschyp with hem on folken wyse.
> (ll. 265–71)

[And then they discovered foul bodily acts and contrived perverse doings against nature, and practised them wantonly upon each other, and eagerly with others too in a wicked fashion. Their flesh became so foul that the devils noticed how very beautiful the daughters of men were, and they had intercourse with them in human fashion.]

Well-known biblical commentators, notably Peter Comestor in his *Historia Scholastica*, make it clear that the poet refers here chiefly to acts of male and female homosexuality. It is this behaviour against the law of nature, 'agayn kynde', that leads on to unnatural copulation with devils, unnatural giant offspring, and finally God's uncontrollable anger.[1]

The identification of 'filth of the flesh' especially with homosexuality is by no means peculiar to this part of *Cleanness*. In the transitional passage which follows his brilliant account of the flood, the poet introduces the second main story as an example of the same kind of wickedness ('this ilk evel', l. 573), and so indeed it proves to be: Sodom and Gomorrah. So far as concerns these first two examples (the third takes a different tack), the argument of the poem could hardly be more offensive to most modern theology and ethics. For one thing, the representation of God as overcome by feelings of anger and even disgust takes to an extreme a tendency observable also in *Pearl* and *Patience*, treating him virtually as if he were just another, albeit omnipotent, character in the story. An angry God is familiar from many Old Testament stories; but this God is also fastidious, even squeamish (ll. 21, 598), and his reactions to sexual 'filth' come very close to physical nausea: 'Me wlatez withinne' (l. 305). The poet himself treats homosexuality with equal disgust, taking his leave of the subject at last with a description of the site of Sodom, now the Dead Sea, as black, stinking, unnatural, and incapable of supporting any life (ll. 1009–48). Medieval Christians, however, did not lack scriptural authority for their homophobia; and the *Cleanness* poet could have pointed to other passages than the Genesis story of Sodom. Thus St Paul, writing to the Romans, recalls God's anger against unnatural sex: 'Their women have changed the natural use into that use which is against nature. And, in like manner, the men also, leaving the natural use of the women, have burned in their lusts, one towards another' (Romans 1: 26–7). It is in keeping with medieval opinion, too, that the poet should present positive examples of heterosexual married relationships, in the persons of

27

Noah, Abraham, and Lot; but he goes further than that, and invents for God a lyrical speech to Abraham in praise of the 'play of paramorez' in marriage (ll. 697–708). God's praise here of passionate sexual love between man and wife (albeit with the light on, l. 706) has an intensity and conviction which might well have surprised contemporary readers more than the intensity of those homophobic sentiments with which it is coupled.[2]

Once the Sodomites have been disposed of under the Dead Sea, an important transitional passage (ll. 1049–148) moves the argument about cleanness forward, and prepares for the third and last main story, Belshazzar's feast. The transition begins with a surprising reference to the *Roman de la Rose* of Jean de Meun, a passage where the lover is advised to conform to the tastes of his beloved: just so, men should win the love of a clean God by their own cleanness. There follows a demonstration of the cleanness of Christ in his life on earth, and a warning against relapsing into sin once one has been purified by penance. Even dishes or vessels that have once been used in church, the poet adds, must never afterwards be put to other uses. It is this last reference to the desecration of holy things that marks a shift in the prime argument of the poem away from sexual uncleanness; for the long ensuing narrative of Nebuchadnezzar and Belshazzar focuses (though with much ancillary matter) upon the fate at their hands of the holy contents of Solomon's temple – vessels, vestments, and other consecrated equipment. This story, like the first, purports to show how God's wrath singles out uncleanness, as against other kinds of sin. Despite the fact that Nebuchadnezzar has conquered and sacked Jerusalem with many atrocities, he dies in his bed. This is because he repented his sins, respected the consecrated purity of the temple contents looted by his men, and acknowledged the power of the God these objects were designed to serve (ll. 1309–28). His son Belshazzar, by contrast, dies a terrible death at the hands of the Medes and Persians, not because of his pride or lechery, we are invited to believe, but because he 'fouled' the Solomonic treasures at his great feast, most especially by letting his concubines drink from the holy vessels. The prophet Daniel explains this at lines 1709–20 (following the Book of Daniel, 5: 23), and the poet reiterates the explanation at the end:

And thus watz that londe lost for the lordes synne,
And the fylthe of the freke that defowled hade
The ornementes of Goddez hous that holy were maked.

(ll.1797–9)

[And thus that land was destroyed because of the lord's sin and the filth of the man who defiled those ornaments of God's house which had been sanctified.]

It cannot be said that tracing the main argument of this poem, as I have been doing, makes *Cleanness* much easier to comprehend today. The poet regards both sexual deviance and the desecration of holy objects as 'unclean': so much is clear. But how are we to understand the connection? One way is to look into other medieval religious writings: moral treatises, sermons, and biblical commentaries. Thus one scholar, Morse, draws particular attention to the idea of man as a vessel which may be either virtuously clean or sinfully dirty, suggesting that Belshazzar's pollution of the temple vessels would have been understood as an allegory of moral corruption. Another scholar, Lecklider, invokes an impressive range of homilies and biblical commentaries to expound *Cleanness* as an Advent poem, based on the liturgy of the church. These approaches tend, however, to concentrate on allegorical readings at the expense of the specific interpretations which the poet himself offers. They tend to generalize the meaning of 'uncleanness', almost as if it just meant 'sin'; but how, in that case, could the poet argue that God punishes the sin of uncleanness more severely than any other? That argument is plainly stated in a passage which distinguishes uncleanness in this respect from other sins (ll. 177–204), and it is supported by the ensuing biblical narratives, as I have tried to show.

An alternative approach to the poet's thinking invokes not medieval homily and exegesis but modern anthropology. Thus it has been shown that the whole range of treatments of sexual uncleanness in the poem can be understood according to a general human rule familiar to anthropologists, that sex should not take place between people either too close to, or too far from, each other (*Companion*, 53–69). In *Cleanness* it is the homosexual partners who, belonging to the same sexual category, whether male or female, are too close to each other, while human and supernatural beings are too far apart. These two rules are broken successively before the flood, first by the homosexuals and then by women sleeping with devils; and in Sodom they are both broken at once, when the men of Sodom try to teach a pair of angels their way of loving (ll. 841–4). A similar, but more comprehensive, analysis of cleanness in the poem may be found in what must be the best essay on the subject, by Spearing. Spearing draws upon a book by the anthropologist Mary Douglas for the idea that cultures attribute impurity to anything deemed to be out of place, outside its proper category – the category being set, for a medieval Christian, by God the creator.[3] This description enables Spearing to show an inner logic in the poem's many and various references to the unclean. 'Unnatural' sex counts, of course; but so does the misuse of sacred vessels for profane purposes. One does not need an anthropologist to tell us that dirt – matter out of place – is unclean; but the wedding guest who turns up, in the parable, with fouled clothes is also polluting a ceremonial occasion. Similar considerations apply to the extraordinary passage on the cleanness of Christ (ll. 1069–109): he came clean from Mary's womb, without the usual mess; he hated to touch anything dirty; he miraculously made sufferers healthy and clean; and he could cut bread with his hand alone, as clean as with a knife. This is the same God who, in the three main stories, purifies a polluted world with storm and sword. Medieval allegorizing interpretations do play a part in *Cleanness*, certainly; but what the poem most characteristically displays, I think, is a deep and spontaneous sympathy with features of Old Testament culture which required no allegorical exegesis to accommodate them to the poet's own values.

However it may be interpreted, *Cleanness* remains something of a loose and baggy monster. Admittedly, comparison with the other three, very tightly constructed, poems would be fairer if editors showed more consistency in displaying the structural divisions which are marked by large decorated initial letters in all four manuscript texts. Just as *Sir Gawain* is divided into four fitts, so *Cleanness* should be divided into three. Its three extra-large capitals, at lines 1, 557, and 1157, mark out roughly equal numbers of lines for its three main examples.[4] Yet the poem does lack the shapeliness of the others (it is the only one not to close on a repetition of its first line). There is a sense that the sheer narrative zest that characterizes all the Cotton Nero poems here submits rather reluctantly to the constraints of theme and form. Thus, one may wonder why almost 200 lines are devoted to the scene between God and Abraham, before the story moves to Sodom. Abraham provides a positive example, of course, but not specifically of cleanness, despite the 'clene clothe' (l. 634) on which he serves the picnic. Similar doubts arise about the early parts of the Belshazzar story. The sparing of Nebuchadnezzar, like the earlier stories of Lucifer and Adam, contributes to the argument, in so far as he, unlike Belshazzar, does not pollute the temple vessels; but why are 150 lines devoted to his siege and destruction of Jerusalem? This passage serves to explain how the temple fell into the hands of the Chaldeans, certainly; but its main moral point – the Jews punished for idolatry – seems a distraction from the main business of the poem.

Yet it is in the narratives that the strength of *Cleanness* lies, in the imaginative recreation of Old Testament events, often sparsely told there. This is not an exercise in the historical imagination, as in Thomas Mann's remarkable *Joseph and his Brethren*; nor, on the other hand, does the poet show any self-consciousness in modernizing the stories. Storms, sieges, and feasts were familiar themes in alliterative poetry, and the poet writes as if these and the other events were present before his eyes. Here, to conclude, are three short examples, first from the account of the flood:

> Bi that the flod to her fete flowed and waxed,
> Then uche a segge segh wel that synk hym byhoved.
> Frendez fellen in fere and fathmed togeder,
> To drygh her delful destyné and dyghen alle samen;
> Luf lokez to luf and his leve takez,
> For to ende alle at onez and for ever twynne.

(ll. 397–402)

[Once the flood had reached their feet and risen higher, every man saw for sure that he was bound to go under. Friends gathered together and embraced, wishing to endure their terrible destiny and die in each others' company. Lover looks to lover and takes his leave, preparing to end all at the same time and part for ever.]

Critics speak of sympathy here, but that seems beside the point. At most, it appears to me, the writer may be said to risk sympathy, in the interests of showing what it must have been like – the water first reaching the men's feet, and then slowly engulfing them. Again, in the second story, the poet imagines what it was about the visiting angels that attracted the Sodomites:

> Bolde burnez wer thay bothe, with berdles chynnez,
> Ryol rollande fax to raw sylk lyke,
> Of ble as the brere-flour, whereso the bare schewed.
>
> (ll. 789–91)

[They were both fine men, with beardless chins, glorious waving hair like raw silk, and their colour like the briar rose wherever the bare flesh showed.]

The description, as one reader has observed, 'seems designed to turn heads', with its poignant sensual detail: 'raw sylk', 'the bare'.[5] Finally, a little cameo from the last story. This is prompted by the single phrase *hac nocte* in the laconic conclusion to the biblical version of Belshazzar's feast: 'The same night, Baltasar the Chaldean king was slain' (Daniel 5: 30).

> The solace of the solempneté in that sale dured
> Of that farand fest, tyl fayled the sunne;
> Thenne blykned the ble of the bryght skwes,
> Mourkenes the mery weder, and the myst dryves
> Thorgh the lyst of the lyfte, bi the logh medoes.
> Uche hathel to his home hyghes ful fast,
> Seten at her soper, and songen therafter;
> Then foundez uch a felaghschyp fyrre at forth naghtes
>
> (ll. 1757–64)

[The pleasures of the great event and splendid feast in that hall lasted until the sun went down. Then the bright sky grew pale, the fine weather becomes murky, and the mist comes driving through the lower air across the low-lying meadows. Everyone hurries quickly home, and they sit at their suppers, with singing to follow; and then, later on at night, every gathering breaks up.]

Darius and his army have already entered Babylon secretly; but everything in the town seems normal, though the night has brought bad weather and a rather sinister mist in the meadows (through which, perhaps, the attackers are moving unseen). The great feast concludes, but the social life of the townsfolk continues, with Babylonians hurrying home to escape the weather, sitting at supper and singing far into the night. The tiny domestic idyll creates a distinctly piercing effect in its context, preceded by a great feast and to be followed by a great slaughter.

5

Patience

Whatever one may think of the other two Cotton Nero poems, *Cleanness* and *Patience* must surely be the work of one hand. They both start by announcing the particular virtue with which they will be concerned, citing from the Beatitudes Christ's promised reward for that virtue. Both go on to illustrate their theme with Old Testament stories, chosen to contrast the cleanness or patience of God with the corresponding vices among men – Jonah, in the case of *Patience*. In both poems, too, the choice of stories and their application to the theme show a similar mind at work, a mind ingenious and independent in its concern, not with allegorical interpretations, but with the varieties of literal moral example to be derived from the old stories.

One does not need to invoke anthropology to explain *Patience*. For modern readers its moral theme is less difficult than that of *Cleanness*. Yet the idea of patience evidently meant more to Ricardian poets than it does today. In Chaucer's *Canterbury Tales*, patience is spoken of as a 'heigh vertu' and a 'greet vertu of perfeccioun' (V, 773; VII, 1517), and it is exemplified by the Clerk's story of patient Griselda – a tale which, the Clerk says, teaches us to receive the adversities that God sends in 'vertuous suffraunce' (IV, 1162). In a central episode of Langland's *Piers Plowman*, again, the hero is a personified Patience, teaching Will to control his exasperation at the hypocrisy of an egregious friar – that virtue being the traditional remedy against such rebellious and angry impulses. Such 'vertuous suffraunce' turns out also to be the best policy, for *patientes vincunt*, patient people end up victorious (as Griselda did). Langland's Patience quotes this prudential Latin maxim several times; yet he is also a charismatic figure, representing patience as a lofty ascetic ideal.

33

So Langland shows the virtue at its fullest extension, claiming for it both spiritual excellence and practical efficacy.[1]

The choice of the story of Jonah and the whale to illustrate the theme of patience is unusual (the standard example was Job). Perhaps the poet's attention was caught by the Book of Jonah's description of God as 'patiens et multae miserationis' ('patient and of much compassion', Jonah 4: 2). In the poem, as in the biblical narrative, God displays his patience and compassion both towards the repentant people of Nineveh and also towards his recalcitrant prophet Jonah. As he remarks to the latter, 'Couthe I not thole bot as thou, ther thryved ful fewe' (l. 521), that is, 'If I were capable of no greater patience than you have been displaying, very few human beings would escape unscathed'. Whereas *Cleanness* showed God mostly as provoked beyond even his endurance by wickedness in his creation, his one act of violence in *Patience* proves to have a beneficent end; for the great storm at sea, so far from destroying Jonah, diverts him back (via the whale's belly) to his prophetic mission and so ensures the salvation of the Ninevites. The poem also invokes, glancingly, the supreme example of patience given in the passion of Christ, when God suffered at the hands of his own creation.[2] In rebellion against God's command to preach in Nineveh, Jonah is represented as imagining that, if he went, he might be stripped naked and 'on rode rwly torent with rybaudes mony' ('Cruelly torn apart on a cross by many ruffians', l. 96). Following his crucifixion, Christ descended for three days into Hell, and this further example of divine suffering is adumbrated in the metaphorical language that the poet uses in describing the whale's belly, which 'stank as the devel' and 'savoured as helle' (ll. 274–5; also 'warlowes guttez' and 'hellen wombe', ll. 258, 306).

Christ himself is said, in Matthew's gospel, to have cited Jonah's three days in the whale as prefiguring his own time in Hell: 'For as Jonas was in the whale's belly three days and three nights: so shall the Son of man be in the heart of the earth three days and three nights'. Hence Jonah took his place among the most familiar Old Testament 'types' of Christ, and the poet could touch off an occasional New Testament allusion to amplify his treatment of the long-suffering of God. But Jonah himself stands as an example of the human opposite. Chaucer's Parson speaks of patience as a 'remedie agayns Ire' (*Canterbury Tales*, X, 659);

and the impatience of Jonah accordingly takes the form of *ira*, rebellious anger against God's treatment of him. It is in the fourth and last chapter of the biblical text that Jonah appears as *iratus*. There he is angry first at God's sparing of the Ninevites, prompting God to ask, 'Dost thou think thou hast reason to be angry?' ('Putasne bene irasceris tu?', Jonah 4: 4); and God asks the same question after Jonah has complained about the destruction of his leafy bower, 'Putasne bene irasceris tu super hedera?', to which Jonah replies, 'I am angry with reason even unto death' (4: 9). So also in the English poem: at the sparing of Nineveh, Jonah 'wex as wroth as the wynde' (l. 410, also 'anger', 'wrath', ll. 411, 431); and at the loss of his bower, he experiences 'hatel anger and hot' (l. 481, also 'wroth', ll. 491, 497). At the beginning of the story, the Bible says nothing of Jonah's reaction to God's command ('And Jonas rose up to flee into Tharsis from the face of the Lord', Jonah 1: 3); but the poet describes his reaction at some length, as the first of three occasions where God provoked him to anger: 'Al he wrathed in his wyt, and wytherly he thoght' ('His mind was filled with rage, and he thought rebellious thoughts', l. 74). Here, as in the later episodes of Nineveh and the bower, Jonah's anger puts him at cross purposes with God; and he deliberately sets off in quite the wrong direction for a traveller to Nineveh.

Jonah's anger finds its most frequent expression in what the poem calls his 'jangling'. After deciding not to go to Nineveh, he hurries away 'ay janglande for tene|That he nolde thole for nothyng non of those pynes' ('angrily grumbling the whole time that he was not at any price prepared to suffer any of those torments', ll. 90–1). Similarly, after witnessing God's sparing of Nineveh, the prophet goes off into the country 'joyles and janglande' (l. 433). 'Jangle' denotes a rather strong form of grumbling; and it has recently been pointed out that two Latin treatises of the time cite Jonah as an example of just such argumentative complaining (*murmur impatientiae*, in the Latin): 'Murmur may occur with respect to the command of a superior; murmuring against his wholesome command is impatient. So Jonah, murmuring against the command of the Lord, is handed over to be devoured by a whale.'[3] In fact, as we have seen, Jonah says nothing at this point in the biblical narrative; but he does 'murmur' later, at the sparing of Nineveh:

And Jonas was exceedingly troubled, and was angry. And he prayed to the Lord and said: I beseech thee, O Lord, is not this what I said, when I was yet in my own country? Therefore I went before to flee into Tharsis: for I know that thou art a gracious and merciful God, patient and of much compassion and easy to forgive evil. And now, O Lord, I beseech thee take my life from me: for it is better for me to die than to live. (Jonah 4: 1–3)

Patience amplifies this speech to fifteen lines of exasperated complaint. God has spared the city for nothing more than 'a prayer and a pyne' ('the odd prayer and act of penance', l. 423) and so made nonsense of Jonah's divinely-inspired prophecy of its imminent destruction. This has turned his prophet into a liar ('les', l. 428). The self-concern in that parting shot introduces a note of comedy, and this becomes stronger in the English Jonah's protests at the destruction of his leafy bower. He first accuses God of deliberately setting out to torment him, and then objects to God's behaviour on principle. The exchange is vividly imagined by the poet. In the Bible, God asks Jonah, 'Dost thou think thou hast reason to be angry, for the ivy?', to which he replies, 'I am angry with reason even unto death' (Jonah 4: 9). In the poem:

> 'Is this ryghtwys, thou renk, alle thy ronk noyse,
> So wroth for a wodbynde to wax so sone?
> Why art thou so waymot, wyghe, for so lyttel?'
> 'Hit is not lyttel,' quoth the lede, 'bot lykker to ryght;
> I wolde I were of this worlde, wrapped in moldez.'
>
> (ll. 490–4)

['Is this reasonable, man, all your fierce talk? to get so quickly angry over a woodbine? Why are you so worked up, man, over so little?' 'It is not little,' said the man, 'but more a matter of justice. I wish I were out of this world, buried in earth.']

This is a fine piece of jangling. Jonah takes the moral high ground: the bower may not have been much in itself; but a point of principle is at stake, and that is no small matter: 'Hit is *not* lyttel...bot lykker to ryght'. What 'right' does Jonah have in mind? He is too cross, surely, to know.

'Is not this what I said, when I was yet in my own country?' The gap which the Bible left at that earlier point in the story is filled in *Patience* with two utterances of angry protest (ll. 75–88 and 93–6). However, the reasons he here gives for declining the

mission are not those he later claims to have given (that he
already knew that God·would relent and make a fool of him).
They are rather less sophisticated: fear of imprisonment,
blinding, and death at the hands of the Ninevites. Thus,
Spearing observes, 'the medieval Jonah convicts himself of a
childish inconsistency'.[4] Inconsistency, for sure, though it is not
only children who make arguments suit their needs in this way.
All Jonah's janglings spring from the same conviction, that God
does not care – not for his reputation as a prophet, not for his
physical comfort in the heat of the sun, and not even for his life:

> 'Oure Syre syttes,' he says, 'on sege so hyghe
> In His glowande glorye, and gloumbes ful lyttel
> Thagh I be nummen in Nunnive and naked dispoyled,
> On rode rwly torent with rybaudes mony.'

(ll. 93–6)

['Our lord sits,' he says, 'in his shining glory on a lofty throne, and will
show very little concern even if I am made captive in Nineveh, stripped
naked, and cruelly torn apart on a cross by many ruffians.']

Like *Cleanness*, *Patience* may be said to belong to the ancient
tradition of 'biblical paraphrase' going right back, in England, to
the time of Caedmon. But paraphrase is a poor term for what is
commonly a process of radical re-imagining in such writings.
The Book of Jonah has only four short chapters, with forty-eight
verses in all, and it displays the qualities noted by Auerbach in
his characterization of Old Testament narrative: 'certain parts
brought into high relief, others left obscure, abruptness,
suggestive influence of the unexpressed'.[5] So, although *Patience*
itself is not long (531 lines), it finds much to amplify and bring
into high relief. At the beginning of the story, after supplying
Jonah's reaction to God's command, the poet devotes 150 lines to
his interrupted voyage, expanding most upon the embarkation
and the ensuing storm – both favourite topics of poetic narrative
at the time.[6] The second chapter of the biblical original
presented a more peculiar challenge. It starts abruptly: 'Now
the Lord prepared a great fish to swallow up Jonas: and Jonas
was in the belly of the fish three days and three nights'; and the
rest of the chapter is then devoted to recording Jonah's prayer of
faith and thanksgiving, paying no further regard to his peculiar
circumstances, until he is suddenly vomited up in the last verse.
In *Patience*, by contrast, the 'belly of the fish' (traditionally a

whale) takes its place among the other marvels lingered over in the Cotton Nero collection – the New Jerusalem, Noah's flood, the Green Knight. As the poet observes, 'Hit were a wonder to wene, yif holy writ nere' ('It would be a wonder hard to believe in, if it were not in the Bible', l. 244). Down in to the whale's huge jaws like a speck of dust blown in through a great church door – 'as mote in at a munster dor' – Jonah slithers down past its gills and tumbles head-over-heels until he comes to a stop, finding his feet in its filthy and stinking stomach. The poet also expands upon the very different kind of 'bower' in which Jonah finds himself later in the story: 'And the Lord God prepared an ivy, and it came up over the head of Jonas, to be a shadow over his head and to cover him' (Jonah 4: 6). What form could such a sheltering growth take? *Patience* imagines it:

> For hit watz brod at the bothem, boghted on lofte,
> Happed upon ayther half, a hous as it were,
> A nos on the north syde and nowhere non ellez,
> Bot al schet in a schawe that shaded ful cole.
>
> (ll. 449–52)

[For it was broad at the bottom and vaulted above, closed in on every side just like a house, with a porch entry on the north side and nowhere any other, but all shut in with foliage giving very cool shade.]

In *Patience*, as in *Cleanness*, the story is told explicitly as a moral *exemplum*; and it is therefore subordinated to the authorial observations which precede and follow it, pressing the claims of patience or 'suffraunce'. These observations combine, quite without embarrassment, a high spiritual claim for the virtue with frankly prudential considerations – as medieval moralists commonly do. The high claim is attributed to Christ, in the poet's version of the eighth and last of the Beatitudes: 'Blessed are they that suffer persecution for justice' sake: for theirs is the kingdom of heaven' (Matthew 5: 10). The poet takes this as referring to patience (*persecutionem patiuntur* in the Latin of the Vulgate) and renders it thus:

> Thay ar happen also that con her hert stere,
> For hores is the heven-ryche, as I er sayde.
>
> (ll. 27–8)

[Blessed also are those who can control their hearts, for theirs is the kingdom of heaven, as I said before.]

As the poet goes on to point out, Christ promised the kingdom of heaven, in so many words, only to the first and last of the eight virtues which he blessed, poverty and patience. Accordingly, the latter is here represented at its most spiritual, as an interior virtue that governs and restrains ('steers') the impulses of the heart. Christ said elsewhere, ' In your patience you shall possess your souls' (Luke 21: 19). This notion of controlling or 'possessing' one's whole inner self represents patience as a general virtue, bearing upon all kinds of human impulse and emotion, not just anger, sorrow, and the like. So, it is said at the end of the poem that one should be 'pacient in payne *and in joye*' (l. 525); and, looking back at the episode of the woodbine bower, one can see that the trick produced a double exposure of Jonah's impatience, not only in his anger at its loss, but also in his uncontrolled joy when it first appears: 'so blythe of his wodbynde he balteres therunder' ('so delighted with his woodbine that he rolls about under it', l. 459).[7]

However, the poet's commentary is otherwise more down-to-earth, and surprisingly so in places. He emphasizes the prudential value of being patient: the virtue pleases God and so wins the kingdom of heaven, but it is also the best policy here on earth. The latter argument is most concisely stated near the beginning of the poem:

> For quoso suffer cowthe syt, sele wolde folwe,
> And quo for thro may noght thole, the thikker he sufferes.
>
> (ll. 5–6)

[For if one is able to endure misfortune, happiness will follow; but if one impatiently fails to endure, one will suffer the more severely.]

The play on the word 'suffer' in these lines cannot be reproduced in modern English. Failure to 'suffer' (bear things patiently) simply increases suffering: it is for those who can 'suffer' that things turn out best (*patientes vincunt*).[8] The poet finds a good example of this principle in the Beatitudes themselves, where patience is linked with poverty; for he himself, he says, is poor:

> Thus poverté and pacyence arn nedes playferes.
> Sythen I am sette with hem samen, suffer me byhoves;
> Thenne is me lyghtloker hit lyke and her lotes prayse
> Thenne wyther wyth and be wroth and the wers have.
>
> (ll. 45–8)

39

[Thus poverty and patience are of necessity playfellows. Since I am stuck with them both, I will have to suffer; so it is easier for me to like it and praise their ways than to turn against them, be angry, and end up worse.]

The poet (whether or not he was in reality poor) has already set an example of such submissive patience, by praising Dame Poverty in the Beatitudes passage – albeit that more spiritual kind of poverty of which Christ spoke ('Beati pauperes spiritu'). Critics have remarked on the discrepancy between such poverty 'in hert' (l. 13) and the poverty of the purse from which the poet claims to be suffering; but the point seems to be a wryly humorous one. Certain liberties have to be taken if one is to praise (let alone 'like') one's troubles.

Poverty was not Jonah's problem; but the poet goes on to imagine a case closer to his. What if, he supposes, my liege lord commanded me to go to Rome? I would have to go anyway, so I might as well go with a good grace; grumbling about it ('grychchyng', l. 53) would simply make matters worse, by annoying the lord. That is what happened with Jonah: by attempting to escape from his mission, he angered God and brought trouble upon himself: 'Thagh he nolde suffer no sore, his seele is on anter' ('Because he was unwilling to suffer any hardship, his well-being is at risk', l. 242).

The second half of the story, once Jonah has reached Nineveh, is more concerned with the destructive consequences of anger and impatience. God could have destroyed the city, just as he did destroy the leafy bower; but, as he points out to Jonah, 'Couthe I not thole bot as thou, ther thryved ful fewe'. Since manuscripts did not employ inverted commas, it is not clear where this final speech of God's comes to an end. The last few lines of the poem must be spoken by the poet, for they refer again to his need to bear poverty with patience; but the preceding lines may be attributed either to him or to God. Either way, they sum up the teaching of the poem in typically down-to-earth language:

> Be noght so gryndel, godman, bot go forth thy wayes,
> Be preue and be pacient in payne and in joye:
> For he that is to rakel to renden his clothez
> Mot efte sitte with more unsounde to sewe hem togeder.
>
> (ll. 524–7)

[Don't be so stormy, man, but go about your business; be steadfast and patient in pain and in joy: for anyone who sets out too hastily to tear up his clothes will have to sit down afterwards with more trouble and sew them up again.]

6

Sir Gawain and the Green Knight

Sir Gawain and the Green Knight is in some ways a distinctly English poem – in its alliterative metre, for one thing, and also in the north-country settings of events at Hautdesert and the Green Chapel. Yet the main literary tradition to which the poem belongs is to be looked for in France. Although King Arthur was originally an insular, British hero, romances of Arthur flourished first and chiefly across the Channel: in the verse romances of the twelfth-century poet Chrétien de Troyes and in the great prose cycles of thirteenth-century France. It is in a world already largely realized by such Continental predecessors that the *Gawain*-poet embeds his own story; and there are many things in that world that he simply takes for granted – general conventions of behaviour, and also particular narrative facts.[1] Thus, I believe he would not have expected readers to be at all surprised, as modern ones commonly are, by the explanation that the Green Knight finally offers for the strange events of the Adventure of the Green Chapel. Morgan le Fay, we are suddenly told, devised the whole affair in order to test the Round Table and terrify Guinevere to death, having learned the necessary magic arts during a love-affair with the enchanter Merlin (ll. 2446-62). The hostility of Morgan towards her half-brother Arthur, his knights, and especially his queen was one of the most familiar established facts in French romance, duly explained there on more than one occasion; and marvels such as the Green Knight and his returning head were not infrequently explained by tracing them back, directly or indirectly, to the book-learning of the mysterious Merlin.[2]

It was from French romance, also, that the *Gawain*-poet derived one of the two main elements in his plot: what is now commonly referred to as the Beheading Game. This bizarre story, in which a man agrees to decapitate a challenger after granting that the challenger may later decapitate him in return, has been traced back as far as an early Irish tale, *Bricriu's Feast*. Though it is hardly the stuff of which normal knightly adventures are made, the story appears more than once in French romances. Most probably the English poet encountered it in one of the continuations of Chrétien's unfinished *Perceval*. Here, the young knight Caradoc takes up a beheading challenge presented by a stranger in Arthur's hall, beheads him, and presents himself for the return blow one year later, again at Arthur's court. The stranger, who turns out to be Caradoc's enchanter father, lets him off with no more than a blow from the flat of his sword.[3] The masterstroke in *Sir Gawain* was to connect the outcome of this adventure with the hero's performance in another test, which he unwittingly undergoes on his way to receive the return blow. In this long central episode, Gawain enjoys hospitality at Christmas in a castle. The poet here draws heavily on the customs and conventions of such episodes in French romance; but his main purpose is to introduce his second main plot motif, for which no precedent has been found there: the so-called Exchange of Winnings. By combining this with the Beheading Game, the poet creates a plot of great elegance and strength, rich in suspense and surprises. He also submits his hero to an adventure more complex and testing than Caradoc's. Like Caradoc, Gawain is tested in the Beheading Game as one of Arthur's knights; but it is as an individual that the Exchange of Winnings tests him, and finds him wanting. The latter episode has understandably interested readers more than the relatively conventional public business of the Beheading Game; but a balanced understanding of the poem, and especially of its equivocal conclusion, requires more appreciation of Gawain's public triumph (for such it is) than is commonly allowed. So, before turning to the complexities of his experiences at Hautdesert, I shall first consider the 'public' adventure.

Morgan le Fay's prime purpose in contriving the Beheading Game, as explained at the end by Bertilak, was 'to assay the surquidré, yif hit soth were | That rennes of the grete renoun of

43

the Rounde Table' ('to put your pride to the test and see whether
it is true, what is said about the great reputation of the Round
Table', ll. 2457–8). In the world of romance, honourable
reputations stand in constant need of maintenance and
vindication, to 'keep honour bright' in the face of frequent
challenges; and the élite corps of the Knights of the Round Table
stands especially subject to such challenge, given the 'great
renown' of their supreme chivalric order. Often the challenge
takes familiar forms – a damsel asking for help, or a knight
wanting to joust – but the Green Knight makes a more
unsettling impression. He is frightening because he is weirdly
green all over, carries a huge axe in one hand, and plays the part
of hostile challenger with such violent relish; but he also carries
in his other hand a sprig of holly as a sign of peace and
goodwill, and he asks of Arthur nothing more alarming than a
'Christmas game' (l. 283). Yet that game is itself unsettling, for
the blows are to be delivered without any resistance being
offered; so the prospects are either certain success if the
challenger dies (and surely he must?) or certain death if he
does not (maybe he won't?). It is not surprising that Arthur and
his men fail at first to respond, prompting the Green Knight to
ask: Is this the great warlike house of Arthur, about which we
hear so much?

> 'Now is the revel and the renoun of the Rounde Table
> Overwalt wyth a worde of on wyghes speche,
> For al dares for drede withoute dynt schewed!'
>
> (ll. 313–15)

['Now all the festivity and renown of the Round Table have been
overthrown by the utterance of a single man, for everyone is cowering
for fear without a single blow offered.']

This provocation so enrages the king that he jumps to undertake
the adventure himself; but Arthur, like a king in chess, is to be
hazarded only as a very last resort; so Gawain steps forward in
his place and is ceremoniously invested with the task. The
formalities here, as Gawain kneels to Arthur and receives the axe
at his hand, mark the moment when the hero is entrusted with
upholding the renown of the Round Table. He is, for the
occasion, its designated representative. Equally formal are the
ensuing exchanges with the Green Knight, where Gawain
solemnly pledges his word, on behalf of Arthur and his knights,

to fulfil the terms of the beheading agreement. These terms are set out, successively, with legalistic precision: Gawain is first to deliver just one blow with the axe; then, if occasion arises, he is to turn up in person on the morning of the next New Year's Day to receive, without resistance, a single return blow, to be delivered in person by the Green Knight with whatever weapon he chooses, and at a place, the Green Chapel, which Gawain has to find for himself (ll. 285–98, 378–85, 392–7, 448–56).

It is a test presenting many difficulties: to strike a man's head off with a huge axe at a single blow, itself a feat of strength and skill; to find an unlocated place by a particular morning; and above all to receive, against all human and knightly instinct, a return blow without offering any resistance. Yet by the end of the story Gawain has fulfilled all these conditions to the letter. He strikes off the Green Knight's head; he 'times his travel as a true man should' (l. 2241), to arrive at the Green Chapel on time; and he receives the return blow on his neck without resistance, though not without flinching. And he survives. His survival is doubly determined: at the Chapel, the Green Knight speaks only of his performance on the three days of the Exchange of Winnings agreement at Hautdesert, to which the three axe-strokes are related; yet the narrative logic of the Beheading Game also demands that the hero, if he submits to the return blow, should be spared and praised for fulfilling his pledged word.[4] Gawain's partial failure in the exchange test, though forgiven by the Green Knight, weighs heavy upon him to the very end, as we shall see; but his unqualified success in the beheading test amply justifies the joy with which his companions greet him on his return to Camelot. The poet by no means simply idealizes Arthur's court: in the opening scene, the men and women there are seen as youthful, playful (at least on festive occasions), and perfectly capable of feeling fear, like the rest of us; but this does not justify dismissing, as some critics do, their reactions to Gawain's return as signs of a shallow frivolity. Gawain himself is deeply distressed by his fault on the third day of the Exchange – so deeply that his distress calls only for Arthur to comfort him, as he courteously does (l. 2513) – yet the honour of the Round Table had not been staked on the exchange test. As far as Camelot is concerned, Gawain has survived, against all the odds, and has succeeded in vindicating on their behalf the high reputation of their chivalric order, as that was publicly staked on the outcome of the Beheading Game. So they have every good reason to laugh for joy, and to adopt the green belt as a fresh addition to the insignia of the Round Table. The belt is to be worn henceforth by all knights of the order as a mark of honour:

> For that watz acorded the renoun of the Rounde Table
> And he honoured that hit hade, evermore after,
> As hit is breved in the best boke of romaunce.
>
> (ll. 2519–21)

[For that was agreed as a battle-honour of the Round Table, and whoever wore it was honoured ever after, as it is recorded in the best book of romance.]

These words conclude the story; yet Gawain himself has declared that he will wear the original green belt as 'the token of untrawthe that I am tan inne' ('the sign of that untruth which I have been found in', l. 2509). So it is time now to turn to what has distressed him: the outcome of the Exchange of Winnings agreement, in which he engaged at the castle of Hautdesert.

The Cotton Nero manuscript divides *Sir Gawain* by means of extra-large capital letters into four sections, known as 'fitts'. The second of these begins, in traditional fashion, with the arming of the hero, as he sets off on his adventure, once the year has come round to November; and the poet takes the opportunity of preparing for the greater complexity of moral issues to come by 'tarrying', as he says, over Gawain's heraldic sign, the pentangle (ll. 619–65). The pentangle, he argues, was a particularly appropriate sign for this knight to carry, because it signifies 'trawthe', truth. This is the very quality, fidelity to the pledged word, which is to ensure Gawain's success in the Beheading Game; but there is more than that to 'trawthe'. To be fully 'true', the passage explains, involves five kinds of excellence, each with its own five: physical (the five senses, the five fingers), devotional (the five wounds of Christ, the five joys of Mary), and moral:

> The fyft fyve that I finde that the frek used
> Watz fraunchyse and felaghschyp forbe al thyng,
> His clannes and his cortaysye croked were never,
> And pité, that passez alle poyntez.
>
> (ll. 651–4)

[The fifth five that I find practised by the man was generosity and companionableness especially, purity and courtesy which never failed, and the supreme virtue of compassion.]

These five fives amount to a high and complex ideal of integrity, whose constituents are all linked together, says the poet, like the lines of the pentangle itself, each one of which either crosses or joins every other.

The rest of the second fitt concerns Gawain's journey into 'strange countries' in search of the Green Chapel, his reception on Christmas Eve at the castle, and his lavish entertainment there. It concludes with his host proposing an exchange of winnings. At this point, Gawain has just been assured that he does not need to set out for the Green Chapel until the morning of New Year's Day itself, for that Chapel, strangely, is 'not two miles from here' (l. 1078); but this appears to present the host with something of a social problem, for there are still three days left of the old year, and all the other Christmas guests are going home. So how is his most distinguished guest to be entertained meanwhile? The host has an idea: Gawain can get up late and relax, while he himself goes out hunting; then, at the end of the day, they can exchange whatever they happen to have acquired. He invites Gawain to 'sware with trawthe' to this agreement, and this the hero happily does. The fitt ends on a note of slightly ominous familiarity with the host and his jolly ways: 'The olde lorde of that leude|Couthe wel halde layk alofte' ('The old lord of that household knew very well how to maintain the festive spirit', ll. 1124–5).

The exchange agreement, then, is to occupy nothing more than the slack interval between a big Christmas house party and the final encounter at the Green Chapel. Unlike the 'game' offered by the Green Knight at Camelot, it really does seem to be no more than a Christmas game. Yet Gawain, here and on each of the two succeeding evenings, is once more pledging his word, plighting his troth, to a covenant; and the poet shows evident interest in what ensues, for he devotes the whole of the third fitt to the events of those last three days of the old year. This fitt is a masterpiece of narrative technique, cross-cutting on each day between the host out hunting and Gawain in his bedchamber, bringing them together each evening for the promised exchange. The host hunts deer, a boar, and finally, on

47

December 31st, a fox, while his wife seductively visits the sleeping Gawain. Seduction scenes of this sort occur also in French romances, where a woman – a damsel, daughter, or wife – makes sexual advances to a knightly guest, often with an ulterior motive;[5] but the three episodes in *Gawain* are quite exceptionally elaborate and subtle. So far as the moral issues are concerned, a line already quoted from the pentangle passage offers some guidance: 'His clannes and his cortaysye croked were never'. Gawain's 'clean' responses to the lady are threatened, of course, by her physical beauty and sexy dressing (especially on the third morning, ll. 1736–41 and 1760–9); and courtesy compounds his difficulties, for it requires him to employ, in declining her advances, such flattering and conciliatory language that she has every excuse for pressing on. Yet he most certainly must not sleep with the wife of an apparently trusting host. How, apart from anything else, could he then fulfil his obligation under the exchange agreement?[6] The shape of the moral dilemma emerges most clearly on the third morning, when

> that prynces of pris depresed hym so thikke,
> Nurned hym so neghe the thred, that nede hym bihoved
> Other lach ther hir luf, other lodly refuse.
> He cared for his cortaysye, lest crathayn he were,
> And more for his meschef yif he schulde make synne
> And be traytor to that tolke that that telde aght.
>
> (ll. 1770–5)

[That noble princess pressed him so hard, pushed him so near the limit, that he had either to accept her love there or else refuse it in an offensive fashion. He was concerned for his courtesy, lest he should be a boor, and even more for the bad outcome if he were to commit sin and betray the man who owned the place.]

In these three scenes, however, the poet mainly devotes his lines not to analysing moral issues but to reporting conversations – the kind of conversations between men and women which in his day were known as 'dalyaunce' or 'luf-talkyng' (ll. 1012, 1529, 927). The joy of such talk is that it can mean anything or nothing, so far as serious sexual intentions are concerned. It is this uncertainty that both Gawain and the lady exploit, for their different ends. To give one example, where the lady is sailing exceptionally close to the wind:

'Ye ar welcum to my cors,
Yowre awen won to wale,
Me behovez of fyne force
Your servaunt be, and schale.'

(ll. 1237–40)

['You are welcome to *my cors* to do as you like; I must of necessity be
your servant, and I shall be.']

It is impossible to translate 'my cors'. In medieval English, as in
medieval French (*mon cors*), the phrase could mean no more
than 'myself, me', with no greater physical suggestion than in
modern 'somebody' or 'nobody'. From the moment Gawain
arrived at the remote castle of Hautdesert, coming from no less a
centre than Camelot, everyone there expressed the highest
gratification at the privilege of entertaining such a distinguished
guest; and the lady can claim to be saying, as his hostess, little
more than that: 'You are very welcome, and I am entirely at your
service.' But in these private bedroom scenes such deference
itself strikes a somewhat equivocal note; and the lady's use of
'cors' could be taken as amounting to an actual invitation.[7] In
response, Gawain meets deference with deference. He cannot
recognize himself, he protests, in the Sir Gawain of whom she
speaks so highly, for he is certainly undeserving of such honour.
It should be he who offers her his service, not the other way
round (ll. 1241–7). This speech is quite typical of the lines of talk
by which Gawain manages to avoid compromising either his
'cleanness' or his courtesy. He is indeed a master of 'clean
courteous talk' (l. 1013) – maddeningly so, one imagines, from
the lady's point of view.

A vein of comedy, running through the whole poem, surfaces
here especially in the treatment of the kisses, received by the
hero as he lies naked under his bedcovers (clearly shown in the
cover reproduction here of one of the manuscript illustrations).
Like love-talking, kisses can mean anything or nothing. The
great French prince, Charles of Orleans, wrote a poem praising
'privy kisses of plesaunce' as against valueless social kisses.[8] The
kiss was a common polite sign of greeting and farewell in the
Middle Ages; so the lady can claim to have meant no more than
that: a farewell on the first day, a greeting and farewell on the
second, and, on the third, a greeting followed by two farewells
(at lines 1796 and 1869). But the circumstances are distinctly

'privy', and Gawain, on the first two days at least, says he accepts the kisses only because he feels bound to obey her commands: 'I schal kysse at your comaundement' (l. 1303, also 1501). So what are the kisses worth, as 'winnings'? When, each evening, Gawain comes to exchange them, as a kind of commodity, against the host's winnings from the hunt, their value comes into question. As a scrupulous observer of covenants, Gawain does his best to reproduce the kisses physically, even kissing the host on the third occasion 'saverly and sadly' ('with relish and vigour', l. 1937). But the host, teasingly, wants to know where he got them from, for their value, he rightly observes, depends on that (ll. 1392–4 and especially 1938–9). Gawain, however, refuses to reveal their source, invoking the precise terms of their agreement: ' "That watz not forward," quoth he, "frayst me no more" ' (' "That was no part of the agreement," he says, "don't ask any further" ', l. 1395).

When Gawain comes to encounter his adversary at the Green Chapel, he is praised for his 'trawthe' in paying over the kisses (ll. 2345–55). No blame attaches to them. By this time, however, the whole question has been quite overshadowed by the event which, occurring on the third and last day of the old year, creates extraordinary turbulence in the poem and, eventually, in its hero. Towards the end of the third bedroom scene, Gawain has successfully kept the lady at bay, and she gives him up, with a sigh and a farewell kiss; but then – as an afterthought, it appears – she asks for and offers gifts by which they may at least be able to remember each other. It is here, when all tension between them appears to have relaxed, that Gawain commits himself to the fault which is later to cause him such anguish, by accepting the lady's gift of her belt on condition that he will not pay it over to her husband that evening. It is made clear that Gawain agrees to this, not because the belt was a compromising love-token (though it was), nor because it was an article valuable in itself (though it was), but because of the magic power which the lady claims for it: it will save his life. So, as the Green Knight later pronounces, he went on to cheat at the last of their exchanges 'because he loved his life' (l. 2368). In this poem, and especially towards its end, fear of death looms large; and it is this, and this alone, that leads the hero to prejudice his pentangular 'truth'.

Perhaps surprisingly, Gawain is represented as feeling no

uneasiness about what he has done until confronted with it the next morning at the Green Chapel. As Jill Mann says:

> Gawain is first made conscious of his fault through its externalisa-tion; while his inner conscience acts as its own imaginary 'audience' in respect of the exchange of blows, it is less vigilant in the apparently more frivolous context of the exchange of winnings. But as soon as he sees himself reflected in the Green Knight's gaze, Gawain acknowledges the stain on his inward worth.[9]

Once he does acknowledge the stain, Gawain indeed blames himself with extraordinary intensity and passion. He has broken his pledged word, and so failed in that quality of 'trawthe' for which his pentangle supremely stands. In a speech of formal self-analysis and confession to the Green Knight, at lines 2378–88, he traces his act of 'trecherye and untrawthe' to his 'cowardyse' in face of death, a weakness which led him to withhold what was due to his host under the exchange agreement ('covetyse'). Such faults, and especially treachery, do indeed strike at the heart of his knightly identity, as displayed to the world in the pentangle which he bears on his shield and chest. Gawain has, in the old phrase, 'blotted his scutcheon'.[10]

It is in the nature of heroes, we know, to blame themselves more severely than ordinary mortals; yet Gawain has something in common with ordinary mortals too. He is rattled. When the Green Knight invites him back to resume his stay at Hautdesert, his response slips into an unknightly tirade against women and their wiles; and when, having first flung the green belt back to its proper owner, he now agrees to accept it, he does so in terms where clerical orthodoxy is touched with wincing self-disgust. He will wear the belt for the rest of his life, he says, as a chastening reminder of 'the faut and the fayntyse of the flesche crabbed,|How tender hit is to entyse teches of fylthe' ('the faulty and deceitful nature of the flesh in its perversity, how ready it is to attract to itself spots of filth', ll. 2435–6). But one cannot evaluate these self-reproaches without also taking into account the judgement of the Green Knight, an adversary who acquires in this final scene a new and impressive authority. In his judgement, Gawain has failed in 'lewté' (an alliterating equivalent of 'trawthe'), but only 'a lyttel'. In fact, he has proved himself overall 'on the fautlest freke that ever on fote yede' ('quite the most fault-free man that ever trod earth', l. 2363). A slight nick on his neck is sufficient punishment for what he has done. Gawain has indeed acquitted himself well, even in his dealings with the lady; and he turns out to need no help from others in facing up to his one fault there. So the Green Knight, and later the court of Arthur, can well afford to be kind. Yet Gawain himself is never, to the very end, shown as taking the comfort they offer him; and readers are left with a sharply contrasting tableau: Gawain confessing his shame to the court and swearing to wear the belt for ever as a 'token of untrawthe' (l. 2509), and the Round Table adopting that same belt as a welcome addition to the honourable insignia of their order. Unlike the pentangle, which has a natural title to its particular moral significance (l. 626), the belt can mean different things to different people – and legitimately so, it would seem.

Sir Gawain and the Green Knight may be said, then, to arrive at an open end, inviting readers to reflect upon the conflicting judgements which it leaves unresolved; yet in another, formal, sense its end is firmly closed, for its last long line is almost identical with its first. The poem began with a fast-forward historical introduction, running from the siege of Troy, via Aeneas and Brutus, to the time of King Arthur; and at its end this sequence is run even more rapidly backwards, from Arthur's day back to the siege: 'After the segge and the asaute watz sesed at Troye' (l. 2525, like l. 1). The result here, as in *Patience* and especially in *Pearl*, is to create an effect of circularity. Perhaps it is not a coincidence that both *Pearl* and *Gawain* characterize their main symbols as 'endless': the pentangle is 'the endeles knot' (l. 630), and pearls, rather more oddly, are 'endelez rounde' (*Pearl* l. 738), both symbols representing kinds of limitless perfection. Both poems, too, consist of 101 stanzas, perhaps suggesting both that one century is firmly closed and that another could begin. Medieval and Renaissance writers not infrequently employ such techniques of 'numerical composition', often with symbolic intentions.[11] It is hard to believe that the readers of medieval manuscripts, which do not number lines, could have identified the last line of *Pearl* as line 1212, or the last long line of *Gawain* as 2525; yet a creator might have seen in these figures a secret source of strength and significance for poems which deal, respectively, in multiples of 12 and 5. The total in *Gawain* derives, not from stanzas with a fixed number of lines (101x12 in *Pearl*), but from 101 stanzas (if they can be so called) of very varying length, ranging from 12 to 37 lines.[12] The poet's technical innovation was to mark off each of these paragraphs of unrhymed alliterative verse with a rhyming 'bob and wheel' (see above, p. 23), enjoying the freedom to place them wherever the narrative seemed to call for some punctuation or comment. The very short line, the 'bob', performs a primarily musical function, easing the transition from the long alliterative lines to the short rhyming lines of the 'wheel'.

In the Middle Ages, Arthurian writings took three main forms. Some covered much of the whole 'matter of Arthur' in encyclopaedic form, as Malory does; others centred on the life of a particular knight, as does Chrétien's *Perceval*; and some confine themselves to a single adventure. The 'lay' of Sir Gawain belongs to this last type. Being strictly and exclusively concerned with the Adventure of the Green Chapel, the poet has every opportunity to treat his single sequence of events with ample narrative detail. In this fulness of detail, indeed, his only rival among medieval English poets is the Chaucer of *Troilus and Criseyde*. The *Gawain*-poet can afford to linger over the New Year festivities at Camelot, the passing of the seasons which follows, social life at Hautdesert, the hunting expeditions of the host, the bedroom visits of his wife, and the final encounter at the Green Chapel. This last scene provides particularly fine examples of the poet's narrative genius, his mastery of what Henry James called 'the scenic art'. Its setting is first seen from Gawain's point of view, as he rides down from the snow-covered hills to the dale with its mysteriously punctured mound – a 'chapel' so precisely described that scholars have, quite understandably, set out to identify it in the border country of Cheshire and Staffordshire.[13] And it is by Gawain that his adversary is first heard, speaking ('Abyde!') and whetting his axe somewhere out of sight, and then seen, whirling out of a rocky crevice and using his weapon to vault over the stream which divides them. Later, after the tension of the return blow, the point of view shifts, and we see the hero through the Green Knight's eyes, as he steps back and gazes with admiration at the young man, now joyfully released from his enforced passivity and leaping to defend himself with sword and shield against any further attack:

> The hathel heldet hym fro and on his ax rested,
> Sette the schaft upon schore and to the scharp lened
> And loked to the leude that on the launde yede,
> How that doghty, dredles, dervely ther stondez,
> Armed ful aghlez; in hert hit hym lykez.

(ll. 2331–5)

[The man stepped back and rested on his axe, planting its shaft at an angle and leaning on the blade; and he gazed at the knight in the clearing, seeing how that brave man stands there boldly and without fear, armed and quite dauntless: it delights him in his heart.]

The Green Knight has more to reveal at this stage, and Gawain has more to suffer before the scene is ended, for this is a story in which the worst moments occur when you least expect them; but how brilliantly this moment of relief and relaxation is captured, especially in the posture of the Green Knight, leaning on his upturned weapon, and in his feeling of admiration, now for the first time glimpsed by the reader, for a fellow knight.

7

The *Gawain*-Poet

Were the four poems in the Cotton Nero manuscript all written by the same person? There will probably never be a final answer to this question. The fact that they all occur in the same manuscript copy proves nothing; indeed, books devoted to the works of a single vernacular author were then very much the exception, not the rule. Somewhat more significant is the fact that they all exhibit exactly the same variety of north-west Midland English, locating their language in a rather small and also thinly populated part of the country.[1] But the geographical distribution of poetic talent is governed by no law of proportional representation: there could have been more than one good writer brought up in that region at about that time; indeed, there must have been at least two, if I am right in believing that another poem in just the same dialect, *St Erkenwald*, was written by someone else.[2]

It may be that thoroughgoing computer-assisted analysis of the texts will provide more definite evidence in future;[3] but current opinion, which in general strongly favours single authorship, rests mainly on observation of similarities in theme, structure, language, and imagery. Considerations of this sort make it very hard indeed to doubt that *Cleanness* and *Patience*, at least, are products of the same mind. They both show the same ingenuity in selecting Old Testament examples to illustrate, *per contra*, specific virtues; and both introduce that virtue as one of those blessed by Christ in the Beatitudes, to which both of them apply the rather singular expression 'aght happes' (*Cleanness* l. 24, *Patience* l. 11). This is one of those verbal parallels between the Cotton Nero poems which can escape the general suspicion attaching to such parallels in alliterative verse, where traditional or 'formulaic' language is always to be reckoned with. Again, *Patience* (but not *Cleanness*) has in common with *Pearl* and *Sir Gawain* a circularity of structure marked by the closing repetition of the first line; and *Cleanness* (but not *Patience*) shares with the other two poems imagery of the pearl, as a symbol of perfect or purified humanity (in *Pearl*, but also in *Cleanness* ll. 549–56, 1067–8, 1115–32, and in *Gawain* ll. 2362–5).[4] Perhaps distinctive, too, is the particular attention paid in all four poems to wonders: the paradisal landscape and heavenly city in *Pearl*, Noah's flood and the destruction of Sodom and Gomorrah in *Cleanness*, the belly of the whale in *Patience*, and in *Sir Gawain* the Green Knight and his returning head.

One may also be persuaded by the concern with acts of moral judgement which strongly marks all four poems. The first three all feature God as the judge, albeit in very different circumstances: in rewarding the innocent pearl-maiden, his justice and his mercy are at one; in bearing with the vagaries of his prophet Jonah, he displays the extent of his merciful patience; but in condemning the sinners in *Cleanness*, he marks the limits of that forebearance. In *Sir Gawain* God hardly figures; yet here the words and actions of the Green Knight, as he emerges as an authoritative judge at the Green Chapel, may be seen to raise similar issues; for he tempers justice with mercy in delivering his all-seeing judgement upon the hero. Gawain is not directly under the eye of God, as are the protagonists of the other poems; but, like them, he finds himself face to face with a power that can look down on him. He is the nearest to a heroic figure that any of the poems get; yet in the end, like the dreamer in *Pearl* and Jonah in *Patience*, he finds himself subjected to a penetrating scrutiny from above and has to struggle to come to terms with what he is told. The vein of comedy which these struggles open up is more marked in *Pearl* and especially in *Patience* than in *Sir Gawain*, but they all have in common that unheroic view of humanity which is so evident also in *Cleanness*. One might object that this was simply a view of mankind common to the Middle Ages as a whole, and certainly it is to be found in other poets of the Ricardian period.[5] Yet the Cotton Nero poems do take a distinctively hard line on the limitations of human understanding, achievement, and behaviour, and on the futility of struggling against the way things are. 'Be not so gryndel', as God says to Jonah (*Patience* l. 524) and the Green Knight says to Gawain (*Gawain* l. 2338). To be 'gryndel' (a word the dictionaries find only in these two passages) is to rage against what cannot be otherwise, to kick against the pricks. It is, one must admit, a deeply pessimistic and conservative vision of human life, so far as this world is concerned.[6]

To think about the four poems as products of a single mind, one does not, of course, need to know the identity of the author; and in fact no one has succeeded in tracing him. He must have been a quite near contemporary of Chaucer, Gower, and Langland. The language of the manuscript marks him (and the copyist) as native to a more northerly part of England than any of them; yet he is certainly not to be thought of as a country cousin to his southern contemporaries. Whether or not he worked in London, as some suppose, he knew as much about the social, intellectual, and literary scene of his day as the Londoners. Alliterative verse may have seemed old-fashioned to them, but the ballade stanza of *Pearl* was the very latest thing.[7] The poet was evidently well-read in French Arthurian romance, the *Roman de la Rose*, and the more recent *Mandeville's Travels* (also in French); and he even shows some signs of acquaintance with modern Italian writers, Dante and Boccaccio. *Pearl* and the scriptural poems show familiarity, not only with the Latin Bible, but also with its commentaries, and he had also read in the fields of theology and ethics.[8]

The varied nature of the poems themselves, and the range of reading that they reflect, have suggested to scholars that the poet may have been some kind of cleric who moved in aristocratic or knightly circles. *Sir Gawain* does not, like Sir Thomas Malory's *Morte Darthur*, read as if it were itself the work of an actual knight; yet it is deeply, though not uncritically, sympathetic to knightly values, and both it and the other more 'clerical' poems display intimate familiarity with the customs and values of courtly society. Hence the attraction of the guess that the poet 'may have been a chaplain in an aristocratic household'.[9] Putter has recently put forward a rather more specific guess, prompted in part by the warning of a historian that 'the Northwest could boast no important seignorial households'. The poet, he suggests, 'was almost certainly a cleric from the north west Midlands – probably a relatively unimportant cleric; perhaps in the service of a nobleman; and, arguably, his patron belonged to the circle of prominent Cheshire courtiers at the royal household in London'.[10] It may be so. In any case, there is remarkably little to be learned from the author's representations of himself in the poems. In all of them he speaks in the first person, as a dreamer, a reader, or a storyteller, without giving much away – nothing, perhaps, except the fact (itself doubtful) that he had a daughter, as a cleric in minor orders might.[11] Nor have attempts to find cryptic allusions to his name in the texts produced any acceptable results: the most recent candidates are members of a Cheshire family, the Masseys, either Hugh or John (*Companion*, 28–31). 'The *Gawain*-poet' is a cumbrous expression, and it would be a relief to set, say, 'John Massey' beside 'Geoffrey Chaucer', 'William Langland', and 'John Gower'; but I doubt whether historians will ever succeed in tracking this particular author down.

Notes

CHAPTER 1. THE BOOK AND ITS AFTERLIFE

1 Edwards gives a good description of the manuscript, *Companion*, 197–219, with reproductions of all twelve pictures.
2 On *The Grene Knight*, see Rogers, *Companion*, 365–72. A recent edition is by T. Hahn, *Sir Gawain: Eleven Romances and Tales* (Kalamazoo, Mich., 1995), 309–35. Sir John Paston (d. 1479) owned a book containing 'the Greene Knyght', perhaps the alliterative poem.
3 *The History of English Poetry*, iii (1781), 107–8 (footnote u), citing *Pearl* ll. 1093–1102, 1106, and 1115, and *Cleanness* ll. 601–4.
4 *The History of English Poetry*, ed. R. Price, i (1824), 17 (footnote 7). On pp. 187–8, lines 20–36 of *Gawain* are cited, with promise of a complete edition of that poem.
5 The poem is printed in Oliver, *Three Variations on the Theme of Harm* (London, 1990). It is discussed by J. Kerrigan, 'Mrs Thatcher's *Pearl*', in A. Torti and P. Boitani (eds), *The Body and the Soul in Medieval Literature* (Cambridge, 1999), 181–99.

CHAPTER 2. *PEARL*

1 An annotated Latin text of *Olympia* with facing translation may be found in J. L. Smarr (ed.), *Giovanni Boccaccio: Eclogues* (New York, 1987), 154–73.
2 I. Gollancz (ed.), *Pearl* (London, 1891), pp. xxii, xlviii. See further E. Wilson, *The 'Gawain'-Poet* (Leiden, 1976), 2–3.
3 On the principle of 'accommodation', see A. Putter, *An Introduction to the 'Gawain'-Poet* (London, 1996), 162–7.
4 'Forma sive modus tractandi est poeticus, fictivus, descriptivus, digressivus, transumptivus, et cum hoc diffinitivus, divisivus, probativus, improbativus, et exemplorum positivus', M. Barbi *et al.* (ed.), *Le Opere di Dante*, 2nd edn (Florence, 1960), 405.

5 See Riddy, *Companion*, 143–55, and J. M. Bowers, *'Pearl* in its Royal Setting: Ricardian Poetry Revisited', *Studies in the Age of Chaucer*, 17 (1995), 111–55.

6 On the *Pearl* stanza, see S. G. Fein, 'The Twelve-Line Stanza Forms in Middle English and the Date of *Pearl'*, *Speculum*, 72 (1997), 367–98.

7 See 'Mourning and Melancholia', in Freud, *On Metapsychology*, Penguin Freud Library 11 (London, 1984), 251–68; cited by D. Aers, 'The Self Mourning: Reflections on *Pearl'*, *Speculum*, 68 (1993), 54–73.

CHAPTER 3. ALLITERATIVE POETRY: AN INTERCHAPTER

1 On the Alliterative Revival, see T. Turville-Petre, *The Alliterative Revival* (Cambridge, 1977); also D. Lawton (ed.), *Middle English Alliterative Poetry and its Literary Background* (Cambridge, 1982).

2 Words beginning with any vowel or diphthong, or with h-, alliterate together. Hence: 'Hit watz Ennias the athel and his highe kynde', where 'Ennias' alliterates with 'athel' and 'highe'.

3 It should be remarked, however, that the same double slanting lines mark the beginnings of stanzas in *Pearl* and of paragraphs in *Sir Gawain*.

CHAPTER 4. *CLEANNESS*

1 See J. K. Lecklider, *'Cleanness': Structure and Meaning* (Woodbridge, 1997), 66–79.

2 See the general discussion by E. B. Keiser, *Courtly Desire and Medieval Homophobia: The Legitimation of Sexual Pleasure in 'Cleanness' and its Contexts* (New Haven, 1997). See also A. V. C. Schmidt, *'Kynde Craft* and the *Play of Paramorez*: Natural and Unnatural Love in *Purity'*, in P. Boitani and A. Torti (eds), *Genres, Themes, and Images in English Literature* (Tübingen, 1988), 105–24.

3 *'Purity* and Danger', in A. C. Spearing, *Readings in Medieval Poetry* (Cambridge, 1987), 173–94, drawing on M. Douglas, *Purity and Danger*, 2nd edn (London, 1969).

4 The divisions are marked by roman numerals in the edition by J. J. Anderson, *Cleanness* (Manchester, 1977), but not in that by M. Andrew and R. Waldron, *Poems of the Pearl Manuscript* (London, 1978). As well as the larger capitals at lines 1, 557, and 1157, there are ten three-line capitals. Together, these divide the poem into thirteen sections, which exhibit significant mathematical relationships, according to D. Crawford, 'The Architectonics of *Cleanness'*, *Studies in Philology*, 90 (1993), 29–45.

5 A. J. Frantzen, 'The Disclosure of Sodomy in *Cleanness*', *PMLA*, 111 (1996), 451–64, cited from 457.

CHAPTER 5. *PATIENCE*

1 For discussion of medieval ideas of patience, see the first three chapters in G. J. Schiffhorst (ed.), *The Triumph of Patience: Medieval and Renaissance Studies* (Orlando, Fl., 1978).

2 On the patience of Christ, compare Chaucer's *Parson's Tale*, *Canterbury Tales*, X, 663–9, and *Melibee*, VII, 1501–4, the latter citing the First Epistle of Peter, 2: 20–4.

3 Cited by E. D. Craun, *Lies, Slander, and Obscenity in Medieval English Literature* (Cambridge, 1997), 85. See his chapter generally: 'Exemplifying Deviant Speech: Murmur in *Patience*'.

4 A. C. Spearing, *The 'Gawain'-Poet: A Critical Study* (Cambridge, 1970), 87.

5 E. Auerbach, *Mimesis: The Representation of Reality in Western Literature*, trans. W. Trask (New York, 1957), 19.

6 See N. Jacobs, 'Alliterative Storms: A Topos in Middle English', *Speculum*, 47 (1972), 695–719.

7 R. Hanna, in *The Triumph of Patience*, 69, cites *Fasciculus Morum*: 'Patientia est quae in prosperis non elevatur, nec in adversis frangitur' ('Patience is that which is neither elated in prosperity nor broken in adversity'). See also F. N. M. Diekstra, 'Jonah and *Patience*: the Psychology of a Prophet', *English Studies*, 55 (1974), 205–17, pp. 209–10, citing Proverbs 16: 32: 'The patient man is better than the valiant: and he that ruleth his spirit [*dominatur animo suo*], than he that taketh cities'.

8 See M. Stokes, '"Suffering" in *Patience*', *Chaucer Review*, 18 (1984), 354–63.

CHAPTER 6. *SIR GAWAIN AND THE GREEN KNIGHT*

1 See especially A. Putter, *'Sir Gawain and the Green Knight' and French Arthurian Romance* (Oxford, 1995).

2 Malory's Arthur reflects 'how his owne sistir [Morgan] was his enemy, and that she hated the quene and sir Launcelot to the deth', *Works*, ed. E. Vinaver, 3rd edn, revised P. J. C. Field (Oxford, 1990), 617. For a penetrating discussion of the 'drama of feminine presences', see G. Heng, 'Feminine Knots and the Other: *Sir Gawain and the Green Knight*', *PMLA*, 106 (1991), 500–14. On Merlin as the ultimate source of marvels in the French Prose *Lancelot*, see

E. M. Kennedy, in W. Rothwell *et al.* (eds), *Studies in Medieval Literature and Languages in Memory of Frederick Whitehead* (Manchester, 1974), 173–84.

3 On the sources, see Brewer, *Companion*, 243–55. The Caradoc story is further discussed, and a version printed, in L. D. Benson, *Art and Tradition in 'Sir Gawain and the Green Knight'* (New Brunswick, NJ, 1965), 16–36, 249–57. See also Brewer, *From Cuchulainn to Gawain: Sources and Analogues of 'Sir Gawain and the Green Knight' Selected and Translated* (Cambridge, 1973).

4 Caradoc is spared by his father. In the *Perlesvaus* version, Lancelot is spared, and praised as 'the most loyal knight in the world' (trans. Brewer, 26). Gawain is also spared in the *Mule Sans Frein* version, 'because he was so loyal and because he had so well kept his promise' (trans. Brewer, 35).

5 Some examples are translated by E. Brewer, *From Cuchulainn to Gawain*, 47–74.

6 The libretto for Birtwhistle's opera *Gawain* invents a curious explanation for the Exchange of Winnings: the wife is actually in love with Gawain, and her husband, knowing this, invents the exchange agreement to ensure that the hero will be deterred from taking advantage of her passion.

7 See the note to l. 1237 in the Tolkien-Gordon-Davis edition.

8 This poem appears in the edition of Charles's English poems by M.-J. Arn, *Fortunes Stabilnes* (Binghamton, NY, 1994), 272–3. For a good discussion of the kisses and their significance in the 'market realities' of the exchange, see J. Mann, 'Price and Value in *Sir Gawain and the Green Knight*', *Essays in Criticism*, 36 (1986), 294–318.

9 'Price and Value', 309.

10 Thomas Lord Darcy said in 1536: 'He that promiseth to be true to one, and deceiveth him, may be called a traitor, for what is a man but his promise?'; quoted by M. James, *English Politics and the Concept of Honour, 1485–1642, Past and Present*, Supplement 3 (1978), 29. On Gawain as an 'honourman', see D. Aers, *Community, Gender, and Individual Identity: English Writing 1360–1430* (London, 1988), 153–78. On 'truth' and 'treachery', see R. F. Green, *A Crisis of Truth: Literature and Law in Ricardian England* (Philadelphia, Pa., 1999), especially the discussion of Gawain's two contracts, 317–21.

11 On numerical composition, see E. R. Curtius, *European Literature and the Latin Middle Ages*, trans. W. Trask (London, 1953), 501–9.

12 The stanza on the five fives of the pentangle, predictably, has 25 lines.

13 See Elliott, *Companion*, 105–17, with maps and photographs.

CHAPTER 7. THE 'GAWAIN'-POET

1 The *Linguistic Atlas of Late Middle English* locates the dialect of the manuscript in either SE Cheshire or NE Staffordshire. Duggan, *Companion*, 240–2, sees some differences between the poet's dialect and the scribe's, locating the former 'further south, in Staffordshire'. For further discussion of matters considered in this chapter, see Andrew, 'Theories of Authorship', *Companion*, 23–33.

2 On *Erkenwald* (a fine poem in its own right), see *Companion*, 26–8, and L. D. Benson, 'The Authorship of *St. Erkenwald*', *Journal of English and Germanic Philology*, 64 (1965), 393–405.

3 See *Companion*, 31–3, and R. A. Cooper and D. A. Pearsall, 'The *Gawain*-Poems: A Statistical Approach to the Question of Common Authorship', *Review of English Studies*, n.s. 39 (1988), 365–86.

4 On pearl-imagery in those poems, see A. C. Spearing, *The 'Gawain'-Poet: A Critical Study* (Cambridge, 1970), 33–6.

5 As argued in J. A. Burrow, *Ricardian Poetry: Chaucer, Gower, Langland and the 'Gawain' Poet* (London, 1971), ch. 3.

6 See Spearing on 'man confronted and baffled by a non-human power', in *The 'Gawain'-Poet*, 29–32.

7 See S. G. Fein, 'The Twelve-Line Stanza Forms in Middle English and the Date of *Pearl*', *Speculum*, 72 (1997), 367–98, especially 393.

8 The most recent discussion of the poet's reading is by A. Putter, *An Introduction to the 'Gawain'-Poet* (London, 1996), 4–14.

9 So E. V. Gordon in the introduction to his excellent edition of *Pearl* (Oxford, 1953), xlii. D. Aers sees *Gawain* as utterly committed to knightly values in his *Community, Gender, and Individual Identity: English Writing 1360–1430* (London, 1988), 153–78.

10 A. Putter, *Introduction to the 'Gawain'-Poet*, 37. The historian to whom he refers, on p. 23, is M. J. Bennett, whose book gives the best account of the poet's native region: *Community, Class, and Careerism: Cheshire and Lancashire Society in the Age of 'Sir Gawain and the Green Knight'* (Cambridge, 1983).

11 See Spearing on 'Poetic Identity', *Companion*, 35–51, arguing that 'the "I" of narration is generically determined' (42). It is a 'nameless and shifting "I"' (44).

Select Bibliography

EDITIONS

Modern Editions

Pearl, Cleanness, Patience and Sir Gawain and the Green Knight, ed. A. C. Cawley and J. J. Anderson (London, 1976). Handy Everyman edition.

The Poems of the Pearl Manuscript, ed. M. Andrew and R. Waldron (1st edn., London, 1978; 2nd edn., Exeter, 1996). The best edition of the four poems together.

The Pearl Poems: An Omnibus Edition, ed. W. Vantuono (2 vols.; New York, 1984). Very full, not very discriminating.

Pearl, ed. E. V. Gordon (Oxford, 1953). The best edition, with excellent introduction and notes.

Cleanness, ed. J. J. Anderson (Manchester, 1977). The most recent helpful edition.

Purity, ed. R. J. Menner (New Haven, 1920). Still valuable.

Patience, ed. J. J. Anderson (Manchester, 1969). The most recent helpful edition.

Sir Gawain and the Green Knight, ed. J. R. R. Tolkien and E. V. Gordon (Oxford, 1925; 2nd edn., revised N. Davis, Oxford, 1967). The standard edition, thoroughly revised by Davis.

Sir Gawain and the Green Knight, ed. T. Silverstein (Chicago, 1984). Fresh and independent.

Other Editions Cited in the Text

Syre Gawayne: A Collection of Ancient Romance-Poems, ed. F. Madden (London, 1839). Contains first full printed text of *Sir Gawain*.

Early English Alliterative Poems from MS Cotton Nero A.x., ed. R. Morris, Early English Text Society, Original Series 1 (London, 1864). First editions of *Pearl*, *Cleanness*, and *Patience*.

Pearl, An English Poem of the Fourteenth Century, ed. I. Gollancz (London, 1891).

FACSIMILE AND CONCORDANCE

Pearl, Cleanness, Patience and Sir Gawain Reproduced in Facsimile, ed. I. Gollancz, Early English Text Society, Original Series 162 (London, 1923).
A Concordance to Five Middle English Poems, ed. B. Kottler and A. M. Markman (Pittsburgh, 1966). Includes *St. Erkenwald* with the four Cotton Nero poems.

BIBLIOGRAPHY

Andrew, M., *The 'Gawain'-Poet: An Annotated Bibliography, 1839–1977* (New York, 1979).
Foley, M., 'The *Gawain*-Poet: An Annotated Bibliography, 1978–1985', *Chaucer Review*, 23 (1989), 251–82. Supplemented for the same period by R. J. Blanch, *Chaucer Review*, 25 (1991), 363–86.
Stainsby, M., *'Sir Gawain and the Green Knight': An Annotated Bibliography, 1978–1989* (New York, 1992).

CRITICAL STUDIES

All Four Poems

Brewer, D., and Gibson, J. (eds), *A Companion to the 'Gawain'-Poet* (Woodbridge, 1997). Comprehensive and up-to-date collection of essays.
Davenport, W. A., *The Art of the 'Gawain'-Poet* (London, 1978). Close readings in the 'new-critical' manner.
Putter, A., *An Introduction to the 'Gawain'-Poet* (London, 1996). Perceptive and intelligent study.
Spearing, A. C., *The 'Gawain'-Poet: A Critical Study* (Cambridge, 1970). Still leads the field.
Stanbury, S., *Seeing the 'Gawain'-Poet: Description and the Act of Perception* (Philadelphia, 1991).
Wilson, E., *The 'Gawain'-Poet* (Leiden, 1976). Quirky, interesting.

Pearl

Aers, D., 'The Self Mourning: Reflections on *Pearl*', *Speculum*, 68 (1993), 54–73. Intelligent use of modern psychology.

Bishop, I, *'Pearl' in Its Setting* (Oxford, 1968). 'Consolation' the main purpose of the poem.

Bowers, J. M., *'Pearl* in its Royal Setting: Ricardian Poetry Revisited', *Studies in the Age of Chaucer*, 17 (1995), 111–55. Associates the poem with Richard II and his tastes.

Duggan, H. N., 'The Metre of *Pearl*', in *Companion*, 232–38. Analysis of its 'iambic tetrameter'.

Fein, S. G., 'The Twelve-Line Stanza Forms in Middle English and the Date of *Pearl*', *Speculum*, 72 (1997), 367–98. Its stanza fashionable in 1375–85.

Gordon, E. V. (ed.), *Pearl* (Oxford, 1953). Masterly introduction.

Kean, P. M., *The 'Pearl': An Interpretation* (London, 1967). Alert to literary and biblical sources and allusions.

Riddy, F., 'Jewels in *Pearl*', in *Companion*, 143–55. The poem as a Ricardian luxury product.

Cleanness

Crawford, D., 'The Architectonics of *Cleanness*', *Studies in Philology*, 90 (1993), 29–45. Numerical analysis.

Frantzen, A. J., 'The Disclosure of Sodomy in *Cleanness*', *PMLA*, 111 (1996), 451–64. On the homosexual theme.

Keiser, E. B., *Courtly Desire and Medieval Homophobia: The Legitimation of Sexual Pleasure in 'Cleanness' and its Contexts* (New Haven, 1997).

Lecklider, J. K., *'Cleanness': Structure and Meaning* (Woodbridge, 1997). Explores sources in biblical and homiletic writings.

Morse, C. C., *The Pattern of Judgment in the 'Queste' and 'Cleanness'* (Columbia, Mo., 1978). On the symbolism of vessels.

Schmidt, A. V. C., *'Kynde Craft* and the *Play of Paramorez*: Natural and Unnatural Love in *Purity*', in P. Boitani and A. Torti (eds), *Genres, Themes, and Images in English Literature (Tübingen, 1988),* 105–24.

Spearing, A. C., *'Purity* and Danger', in Spearing, *Readings in Medieval Poetry* (Cambridge, 1987), 173–94. Brilliant application of anthropological ideas.

Patience

Diekstra, F. N. M., 'Jonah and *Patience*: The Psychology of a Prophet', *English Studies*, 55 (1974), 205–17. Shrewd and informative.

Hanna, R., 'Some Commonplaces of Late Medieval Patience Discussions: An Introduction', in G. J. Schiffhorst (ed.), *The Triumph of Patience: Medieval and Renaissance Studies* (Orlando, Fl., 1978), 65–87. On medieval understandings of the virtue.

Scattergood, V. J., '*Patience* and Authority', in A. J. Minnis, C. C. Morse, and T. Turville-Petre (eds), *Essays on Ricardian Literature in Honour of J. A. Burrow* (Oxford, 1997), 295–315. On the conservative ethos of the poem.

Stokes, M., 'Suffering in *Patience*', *Chaucer Review*, 18 (1984), 354–63. On varieties of 'suffering'.

Williams, D. J., 'The Point of *Patience*', *Modern Philology*, 68 (1970), 127–36. Concise and to the point.

Sir Gawain and the Green Knight

Aers, D., '"In Arthurus Day": Community, Virtue, and Individual Identity in *Sir Gawain and the Green Knight*', in Aers, *Community, Gender, and Individual Identity: English Writing 1360–1430* (London, 1988), 153–78. Emphasis on knightly values.

Benson, L. D., *Art and Tradition in 'Sir Gawain and the Green Knight'* (New Brunswick, NJ, 1965). Wide-ranging and pioneering study.

Borroff, M., *'Sir Gawain and the Green Knight': A Stylistic and Metrical Study* (New Haven, 1962). Thorough and penetrating.

Brewer, E. (trans.), *From Cuchulainn to Gawain: Sources and Analogues of 'Sir Gawain and the Green Knight'* (Cambridge, 1973). Collection of translated texts.

Burrow, J. A., *A Reading of 'Sir Gawain and the Green Knight'* (London, 1965). An early critical study.

Elliott, R. W. V., *The 'Gawain' Country* (Leeds, 1984). The local topography and landscape of the poem.

Green, R. F., *A Crisis of Truth: Literature and Law in Ricardian England* (Philadelphia, Pa., 1999). Valuable on 'trawthe'.

Heng, G., 'Feminine Knots and the Other: *Sir Gawain and the Green Knight*', *PMLA*, 106 (1991), 500–14. Strong feminist reading.

Loomis, R. S. (ed.), *Arthurian Literature in the Middle Ages* (Oxford, 1959). The standard handbook.

Mann, J., 'Price and Value in *Sir Gawain and the Green Knight*', *Essays in Criticism*, 36 (1986), 294–318. 'Mercantile' values in the poem.

Putter, A., *'Sir Gawain and the Green Knight' and French Arthurian Romance* (Oxford, 1995). Illuminating comparisons.

Other Reading

Bennett, M. J., *Community, Class, and Careerism: Cheshire and Lancashire Society in the Age of 'Sir Gawain and the Green Knight'* (Cambridge,

1983). The local historical context.

Burrow, J. A., *Ricardian Poetry: Chaucer, Gower, Langland and the 'Gawain' Poet* (London, 1971). General comparative study.

Douglas, M., *Purity and Danger: An Analysis of the Concepts of Pollution and Taboo*, 2nd edn (London, 1969). Helps with *Cleanness*.

Keen, M., *Chivalry* (New Haven, 1984). Full and sympathetic.

Lawton, D. (ed.), *Middle English Alliterative Poetry and its Literary Background* (Cambridge, 1982). Useful essays.

Mathew, G., *The Court of Richard II* (London, 1968). Vivid and genial study.

Muscatine, C., *Poetry and Crisis in the Age of Chaucer* (Notre Dame, Ind., 1972).

Salter, E., *Fourteenth-Century English Poetry: Contexts and Readings* (Oxford, 1983). Fresh and informative.

Scattergood, V. J., and Sherborne, J. W. (eds), *English Court Culture in the Later Middle Ages* (London, 1983).

Spearing, A. C., *Medieval Dream-Poetry* (Cambridge, 1976). Study of the genre.

Turville-Petre, T., *The Alliterative Revival* (Cambridge, 1977). Valuable study of the 'revival'.

Index

Abraham, 25, 28, 31
Arthur, King, 42, 43, 44, 45, 52, 53
Auerbach, Erich, 37

Belshazzar, 25, 28, 29, 31, 32
Bertilak, *see also* Green Knight, 43,
   47, 48, 50, 51
Bible:
   Genesis, 26, 27
   Psalms, 10–11
   Proverbs, 61
   Daniel, 28, 32
   Jonah, 34–8
   Matthew, 13–14, 25–6, 34, 38–9,
      40
   Luke, 10, 15, 25, 39
   Romans, 27
   I Peter, 61
   Revelation, 9–10, 11, 13, 14, 15
Birtwhistle, Harrison, 4, 62
Boccaccio, Giovanni, 6, 7, 57
Bricriu's Feast, 43

Caedmon, 37
Caradoc, 43, 62
Charles of Orleans, 49
Chaucer, Geoffrey, 22, 57
   Book of the Duchess, 6
   Canterbury Tales, 1, 11, 12, 21,
      33, 34, 61
   Parliament of Fowls, 18
   Troilus and Criseyde, 53

Chrétien de Troyes, 42, 43, 53
Cleanness, 1, 2, 3, 12, 15, 22, 23, 24–
   32, 33, 34, 37, 38, 55, 56
Comestor, Peter, 27
Cotton, Sir Robert, 2

Dante Alighieri, 57
   Divine Comedy, 5, 6, 9, 10, 11
   Letter to Can Grande, 10
Darcy, Thomas Lord, 62
Douglas, Mary, 30
Duggan, H. N., 22, 63

Fasciculus Morum, 61
Freud, Sigmund, 17

Gawain, Sir, 43–54, 56, 57
Gawain-Poet, 55–8
Gollancz, Sir Israel, 3, 6
Gower, John, 1–2, 22, 57
Green Knight, 1, 38, 42, 44, 45, 47,
   50, 51, 52, 53–4, 56, 57
Grene Knight, The, 2
Guinevere, 42

Harsent, David, 4
Hunt, Holman, 3

James, Henry, 53
Job, 34
Jonah, 1, 19, 33–40, 56, 57
Joyce, James, 13

69